Unstoppable Enthusiasm

Habits to Build & Sustain Your Enthusiasm

written by
Matt Powers

Copyright © Matt Powers 2019-24
All Rights Reserved
ISBN 978-1-7321878-6-3
Printed in China on recycled paper
Published by PowersPermaculture123/Matt Powers

Dedicated to the love of my life, my wife, Adriana.

Contents

1	Enthusiasm Unlocks Your Power
17	What Held Me Back
31	The Benefits of Enthusiasm
47	The Roots of Enthusiasm
54	The Daily Habits of Enthusiasm
102	Enthusiastic Action
120	Enthusiastic Thinking
132	Bouncing Back
147	One Last Thing (Maybe Two)
150	Continuing your Education
152	References
153	Acknowledgments
154	About the Author

Enthusiasm is the mother of effort, and without it nothing great was ever achieved.
~Ralph Waldo Emerson

Enthusiasm Unlocks Your Power

The cancer was back...

Twelve years ago it took her thyroid, then melanoma took shark bites of her thigh after the first radiation treatments. A few years later, melanoma returned, and again a few years after that. Then it was basal cell carcinoma more recently, and now a growth the size of a jumbo lima bean in her jawbone.

At first, we avoided the obvious in hopes that it was a bone cyst as the dentist suggested it might be, but those don't destroy bone and teeth roots, and this was. When I explained this to my wife, Adriana, she grew upset, and we ended up arguing about how we were going to talk about it moving forward. The stress levels only rose higher as we waited weeks upon weeks for the appointment with the oral surgeon.

She made the mistake of googling jawbone cancer and clicking on the images option; after that, the fear of cancer and surgery became the implicit theme of our lives. She was already fighting skin cancer on her ear when we learned about her jaw, so it was gasoline on a kitchen fire, and I was feeling helpless for the first time in many years — it was just like years ago when everything fell apart the first time, so I began at the beginning again: I started to research cancer therapies. The rabbit hole has grown considerably longer, more divergent, and complex in the past decade since I started studying. There's an overwhelming amount of information: go vegan, juice, fast, use cannabis, use turmeric, use machines, or use your mind. It almost seems impossible that so many miracle cancer cures exist — how can there be so many pathways to healing? I began to dig in deeper, get more specific, and find actual people who have healed themselves.

What I discovered was nearly all were miraculous faith healings. I watched a video on Youtube of one woman who had been diagnosed with stage four bone cancer declare how it was her absolute faith that healed her: "Mine is included!" she declared, meaning her healing was included when it was said that Jesus Christ healed ALL. It was her conviction, her faith, that healed her. The healing was already there waiting for her — the possibility of it was always present. It was her state of mind that changed — this woman had gone to a faith healing conference and left transformed by it. Was this just a fluke though?

When blessings are given, it is said that the faith of those to be healed is as important or more important than the healer's faith. Even medical procedures are greatly affected by the patient's outlook, and this has been known for a long time. In my research, I discovered <u>You Are The Placebo</u> by Dr. Joe Dispenza, and realized that all the cancer modalities, faith healings, shamans, prophets, blessings, and visions all worked along the same lines: the placebo effect. I also realized that it was the most powerful avenue for change in our lives: it could kill us or heal us. By just believing we have cancer, we can get cancer and even die. By just believing an inert *sugar pill* is a cure, we can get better by taking it — it is by our faith that we are healed. It's miraculous, but for some reason, I grew up thinking of the placebo effect as a weakness. I thought it was a sign of gullibility but revised that thought as I began to study and practice meditation, breathing, and visualization on a daily basis.

I also started to research HOW all these alternative cancer methodologies had actually been carried out. I learned in my work in permaculture that knowing HOW experiments were conducted and presented determined whether their results were trustworthy. I became increasingly open about what my wife was facing, much to my wife's irritation. We both were inundated with messages and emails, each one often pages long on obscure healing modalities, but it led to numerous discoveries as I sifted through them all. I read about how turmeric was fighting cancer in high doses, and I found the exact product online that researchers used in testing. Just one of *Terry Naturally's* turmeric pills is 500x stronger than a single powdered turmeric pill. I also figured out that while Rick Simpson Oil (RSO), whole plant cannabis oil, has been proven to work well superficially (topically) on melanoma, there was no proof that it could reach into the bone.

Discovering DMSO (dimethyl sulfoxide), the chemical solvent often used with arnica to reach deep into the joints to provide relief, was a very fortunate twist of fate. Combining it with the RSO, I reasoned that we could reach the tumor. Adriana's naturopathic doctor also recommended activated oxygen cream which we alternated with the RSO. Cordyceps, Reishi, and Lion's Mane mushroom tinctures were added to her daily routine — all of which have been shown to fight cancer and support the immune system in research. On top of all of this, we began to feed her body instructions, much like Marisa Pears talks about: feeding positive instructions and being meticulous with our words and thoughts. Adriana used a small script she read aloud, telling her body precisely how it was healing and shrinking the growth in her jaw. I would also say that it was shrinking to her and to myself in prayer, meditation, and throughout my day.

While keeping up the regular routine was a dance on its own that led sometimes to conflict, I knew that it was not going to be enough. We had to get over the fragility, the fear, and the fighting — we had to enter growth, healing, and love. I knew that it was enthusiasm, the exact opposite emotion of the fear we were both feeling, that we needed most at that moment. I could not despair — I had to leap. I could not falter. I had to rise with a steadfast gaze fixed on my goal, not with fight, anger, or fear, but with blazing glorious joy and gratitude. I had to transcend the feeling of being overwhelmed and reprogram myself to be filled with Unstoppable Enthusiasm to power not just myself but my entire family out of despair and deep into healing and gratitude. I also knew that I was weak, tired, and overworked, but I was the dad, these were my boys, and this was my wife. I decided to figure it out.

Before we get to what happens next, I want you to ask yourself: what do you think happens next? It's bone cancer - it's not small and it's her sixth encounter with cancer. What would you become in this situation?

Fast forward to over a month later, Adriana is driving off, after a prayer, to the oral surgeon appointment. While I focused on the appointment as she left, I quickly lost myself in my work as the day progressed… then her phone call ripped me from my detached busywork and back into the present moment. I could tell instantly by her shaking voice something had happened and by her, "Guess what?" that it wasn't bad. I began screaming as she told me it had shrunk to the size of a pea, more than two-thirds of the tumor had shrunk, and the surprised doctor no longer wanted to do a biopsy. Instead, he encouraged us to continue our hodgepodge protocol of protocols. *The Impossible IS Possible!*

Even now as I write this, giggles and waves of joy bubble up inside me. I have figured out that every protocol's efficacy is directly related to enthusiasm. Recognizing my wife's enthusiasm was inseparably connected to my own, I realized my transformation was her transformation. While I always knew how influential I was, I didn't realize how responsible I actually was or how closely tied our immune systems and enthusiasm were.

What happened between points A and B at this time in our lives is what everyone needs to hear because this isn't a story about alternative therapies or even miraculous healing, this book is about unlocking our real power — the primary energy powering all healing, success, joy, and love.

Magical, Mysterious, & Moving

> Every person is enthusiastic at times. One person has enthusiasm for 30 minutes; another has it for 30 days, but it is the person that has it for 30 years who makes a success of life.
> ~Edward Butler George

Enthusiasm is the secret sauce of life. It saturates the most exciting times of our life, it exudes from us in defining moments of performance, and it has the ability to pull us out of the fog of depression and fear. Enthusiasm leads us back to our path of purpose and gives us the determination to make it through hard times. Enthusiasm in simplest terms is the spirit of life — it's what makes us feel ALIVE, and when we feel alive, we cannot help but encourage others to feel the same or reflect on how they would go about finding a similar joy for life. Enthusiasm is the common thread woven through all religions, philosophies, education, performance, medicine, business, persuasion, attraction, mindset, and happiness.

This book is your guide to unlocking, training, and sustaining your own personally tailored Unstoppable Enthusiasm. Everyone can retrain their brain to feel less and less pain and more and more enthusiasm. Even as I write this I can close my eyes and experience waves of joy and enthusiasm because I've put in the time and training. This book will guide you on your path to unstoppable enthusiasm. Sourcing personal experience, research, interviews, and studies, this book is an organized framework designed to help you build your unstoppable enthusiasm strategically morning, day, and night from now on, and not some frantic, feverish, or fake energetic mask, but a sustained connection to your authentic enthusiasm.
Soon, you'll be in a new rhythm with a new passion and excitement for life. What's more is it is a gift you have given yourself. You took the time to

figure things out and open yourself up to what you really want and then it flooded into you. Again and again, you did this, until you memorized it like the way you brush your teeth, cross your arms, or wash your hair. You do it everyday morning, day, and night — it's automatic and part of who you are. You ARE Unstoppable Enthusiasm.

Are They Listening to the Music or to the Enthusiasm?

After years of competition, performance, intensive study, and teaching in a variety of settings, it occurred to me that my students and the audiences I performed for were always primarily watching my enthusiasm at work. I realized it wasn't my music or the subject matter they were interested in, they were there to get charged by my charge, and that's the real gift I'm giving: the transmission of this energy from one person to another. This exuberance, it is beyond thinking and doing: it is BEING. The energy is the actual communication — not the medium.

Enthusiasm can be quiet, deeply grateful, steadfastly present, and incredibly peaceful, but it also can radiate from your infectious smile, emanate from exuberant activity, and pour from the mouth in a rapid stream of jumbled words. Enthusiasm's full spectrum focuses on being one with the moment in joy, gratitude, and faith for the future, but we each express these emotions differently at different times.

But is Enthusiasm Quantifiable — is it Scientific?

This book will dig down and uncover the key indicators of what unstoppable enthusiasm is and how you can build the habits to support it, but before we do that, let's define *Enthusiasm*. Originally, it was *En Theos* or *In God*, and it meant having the spirit of God or the power of divinity manifest in us or in our actions. This is still likely the best definition. Later it was associated closely with religious zeal, sometimes bordering on irrationality. This is not the current, nor my, definition, but its influence is still found in many definitions. The most common definition today though is the most mundane: *keen, excited interest or passion in something.*

One of the core purposes of spirituality and religion is to generate enthusiasm in people — to facilitate them living their lives embodying the divine. This could be living the teachings of Jesus Christ, Buddha, Lao Tzu, the Dali Lama, and many others. It could even be a combination of them as recognition has grown that all religions and philosophies have something to teach us, or else they would not resonate and stick around — even if they are "wrong" to you, they point to an unmet need in those folks which is universal and can be understood. I believe we are all reaching for enthusiasm, for our own personal relationship with the divine within us.

We All Need Enthusiasm Now More Than Ever

I need it. You need. We all need Enthusiasm with a capital E! It animates the moments of our day, and the opposite is also true: being unenthusiastic robs us of joy. Instead of a rainbow of possibility, we see a world drained of color, and we recognize everything that reinforces that particular perspective: the news, the climate, gossip, things going wrong in our lives, and even aches and pains in our bodies that we wouldn't have noticed or manifested. We notice the negative when we are lacking enthusiasm, but thankfully, we notice the positive all around us when we embrace enthusiasm, but it starts with the intention to highlight, share, or generate the positive things we want to see in the world.

Enthusiasm differs significantly from exuberance which implies being more energetic behaviorally than other people, usually starting from a young age. Exuberance is studied academically and is considered inborn to a degree. Enthusiasm is quite different. We all have the capacity to develop our enthusiasm. We all can find within us a place of peace, joy, gratitude, faith, anticipation, and excitement. Interestingly, we can't feel gratitude and fear or anger at the same time — gratitude will push them out of our heart and mind if we can focus on gratitude enough to feel it emotionally.

It is a curious fact that our brains cannot tell the difference between a simulated experience and a real one — if we think about something arousing, we tend to respond — sometimes we may even physically respond. If you think about certain foods, can you have a physical reaction from thought alone? What about imagining biting into a freshly cut lemon slice? Can you imagine that? Can you feel the physical reaction in your mouth to your mind thinking about chewing that sour juicy lemon? What if you think about something awful? I won't suggest anything — don't worry, but what happens? Does the pit of your stomach drop? Does an uncertain feeling settle onto the back of your neck? You may even feel pain — I certainly get stomach pain when arguing or thinking negatively about myself or others. If we can think thoughts that arouse us, make us hungry, or even cause ourselves physical pain, what are we doing every day with our thoughts? Are we thinking intentionally? Are we exercising our minds and bodies, so we can grow strong in the ways we desire?

If you are anything like most of us (like me), you are constantly barraged with uninvited thoughts. They just show up with all sorts of demands, worries, fears, and, often, poor suggestions. One of the best pieces of advice I ever heard was: don't believe everything you think. We can circumvent these negative thoughts by directing and training our minds. Now you may ask yourself: what about inspiration, doesn't that come in the form of an interruption too? The still small voice of inspiration comes to us often when we least expect it and often when we are quiet and still. This listening aspect of inspiration is key, and we can hear that difference: the uninvited thoughts differ significantly from welcome inspiration when we take the time to listen carefully. Often the uninvited thoughts are negative, fearful, and selfish. But wait now, does that mean only inspired thoughts feel welcome? Well… let me explain with a story from my life.

When I was a young boy, I only wanted one thing: to grow up to be a rockstar. Now while we can likely debate how close I got to that dream, I did get to play for several years with many famous musicians and their backing band members live, in studios, and on albums recorded in world-class studios with extravagant vintage gear. I've jammed with Billy Gibbons of ZZTop, 45 minutes after meeting him for the first time, live on stage at SXSW, the music festival in Austin, TX. I was living the life — limousines picked me up and dropped me off, one of the members of Bass Players Brunch in NYC had officially invited me, and I had arrived as a professional musician in my mind. Little did I know that I'd soon be quitting The Cringe and leaving NYC, the only place on earth I wanted to live.

Adriana's first bout with cancer was the most catastrophic. We'd just celebrated James' first birthday, and we'd been working with doctors trying to figure out why Adriana was having trouble with extreme exhaustion. I was told by the surgeon in the middle of the operation that she had thyroid cancer, and they were going to remove it and her entire thyroid. They followed that up with radiation, not chemo as so many folks assume. She didn't lose her hair. She did get an aggressive flareup of skin cancer, melanoma, a few months later that nearly reached her lymph nodes and required more extensive surgeries.

At this point, she'd had cancer surgery three times in four months. When she told me she wanted to move to California to recover with her folks, we prayed about it. The still small voice said it was the right thing to do, but I was afraid for so many reasons. It was my identity. It was my best income up to that point — $200-350 an hour to play bass!! It was my known and familiar landscape where I was a young prince of promise living out a childhood fantasy. It was like giving up smoking cigarettes to be honest! I didn't do a great job of it at first — I continued to play for The Cringe when I was in CA for months after we left. They would fly me out to play — the limousine would limp down Grandpa Joe's broken, dirt road in the foothills to get me. I eventually had to find my own replacement to finally remove myself, but it was like leaving a family. I'd played with John

Cusimano for over seven years before he'd ever met Rachael Ray (who used to read over all my writing), and he (and later they) took care of me and were incredibly loyal and supportive friends. When they got married in Italy, they flew us all out for it. I felt like I was turning my back on my adopted family. The entire band and touring crew were very close, but I knew this is what my wife and our young family needed in my heart, so I took a leap of faith.

Ironically, it led to working with the best band I'd ever played with, People with Jimmy Young, and my own national tour with that same band backing me. It also led to me eventually quitting full-time music, spending my time closer to home, and eventually to teaching, gardening, and permaculture. It all came from listening to that still, small voice. Since we left NYC, all our major decisions are decided through entering that space: prayerful listening. Only from that wellspring can we hear the song our deepest heart of hearts wants to sing with all the enthusiasm we can hold without bursting.

Against All Odds

Can enthusiasm hold up in more trying circumstances? Giving up my music career was hard but not truly painful when compared to surviving the horrors of war or even facing the loss of a loved one. During WWII, there were troops of Girl Guides imprisoned in concentration camps all over Europe and in Asia. Over two dozen of these courageous girls were even documented sneaking food, medicine, and clothing to those imprisoned in Auschwitz, one of the most infamous and dreadful Nazi concentration camps, and this was not an isolated phenomenon. Girl Guides were courageous, smart, and selfless wherever they were all over the world — this is why the British government and military relied upon them as messengers over boy scouts. Even the imprisoned guides were unflagging in their determination to both serve and resist. Their enthusiasm, courage, and kindness greatly shielded the Girl Guides from the horrors around them. The guides relied upon their faith, their invigorating habits, and their patterns of kindness, and, in some circumstances, it changed how they all were treated by their captors and how they experienced confinement.

> "One of the things we sang when the Japanese were marching us in to concentration camp was the first verse of psalm 46: *God is our refuge, Our refuge and our strength* - and on it goes - *in trouble we will not be afraid*. All of these words just sung into our hearts. That sticks. It's like you've got a groove sticking in the gramophone record: *I am safe I am safe I am safe*. That was just profound"
> ~Mary, WWII concentration camp girl guide

Their cheery dispositions were well trained — they had the mental and emotional muscles to hold themselves together during their internment.

What prisons are we in today? Are they prisons we've created ourselves? Are they built out of our choices? Are we holding the bars? What if we could live like there were no bars — even if there really are?

Your Best Self

You're loose, open, excited, present, steeped in the growth mindset, and maybe even a bit physical - your heart rate might be elevated. Smiles crescendo but never slip from your face. Your eyes sparkle. You're ready for anything and excited to be your most present self. All your senses are active and charged yet you're centered and in touch with the peace, gratitude, and joy within. You are your best self. You can see clearly. You can feel energy all around you, within you, on your skin, rising up your scalp, and shining from your face. Your chest and chin lift, and you breathe deeply. You feel flushed with the energy of the moment - you are ALIVE!

We all want this. We all need this. We all deserve to become this and cultivate a lifetime of moments steeped with unstoppable enthusiasm. Despite distraction, enthusiasm keeps you focused & shielded from negativity and doubt. Enthusiasm grants us our best days, biggest wins, and best life.

The Stakes Have Never Been Higher

Political upheaval, corruption, climate change, inequality, hunger, racism, personal loss, and betrayal — there are powerful reasons for despair, but do we accomplish anything when we let them wound our hearts, slow our hands, or dull our compassion? Who will lift hearts and minds if we all cave to depression? Who will reset that which is broken? Who will find the new path out of the darkness and into the light again — and for some, perhaps, their first time witnessing it. With so much of our world in darkness, it is up to us who can see the light, no matter how dim or distant, to help others towards that hope and freedom because there is no doubt that we are enslaved when we fall prey to despair. It is up to us to choose to be greater than our fears.

Uncertainty

Enthusiasm is also the antidote to uncertainty. It may not lead to instant action but it will put you into position to receive certainty. Your centered and grateful acceptance of the moment opens you to the next step. There is a drive to know everything, to know it quickly, and to act — there's a sense that we are always running out of time, or that opportunities are constantly passing us by, but what if the opposite was true: time is always waiting for us to use it wisely, and opportunities to improve ourselves and the world around us are everywhere all the time. Uncertainty is a perspective that blinds us to possibility in the guise of being wooed by too many choices or unclear outcomes. When we look within, to our heart, we can see the direction clearer, even when it is a painful or difficult choice, but often, when we are enthusiastic, we perceive an alternative route that, during our uncertainty, we couldn't access. Uncertainty and creativity are two paints that don't mix. We have to let go of uncertainty to allow creativity the room to act, and enthusiasm is creativity's greatest facilitator.

Fear Itself

> We have nothing to fear but fear itself.
> ~Winston Churchill

Uncertainty is actually a mild form of fear. In many ways, enthusiasm is the opposite of fear — you are excited, grateful, and happy to be there: you aren't afraid in the slightest. You are ready for action — not paralyzed by fear. You see the dangers. You acknowledge them, take them into account, and then plot your course with confidence anyway. There is a deliberate nature to your actions, thoughts, and words, and everyone around you benefits from it. You ground those around you with your enthusiasm.

When we are brave, we inspire others to leave their own fears behind. Inside a concentration camp in China, Girl Guides used music, smiling, and their Girl Guide protocols and curriculum to stay safe, maintain their enthusiasm, and keep fear at bay.

> We sang our song yesterday and it went:
> We might have been shipped to Timbuktu
> We might have been shipped to Kalamazoo
> it's not repatriation
> nor is it yet starvation
> it's simply concentration in Shi-foo
> ~Janie Hampton, author of *How Girl Guides Won the War on Reply All*

There are really only two types of fear: fear of loss and fear of pain. Everything fits into these two categories: death, humiliation, failure, betrayal, etc. Enthusiasm is the opposite — it is expectation and anticipation of growth and enjoyment in the moment. If we can hold onto our habits, we can maintain our enthusiasm even in the worst of times and places.

Negative News

Protecting our minds and hearts has always been important, but today it's even more critical. Marketing has long relied upon what works, and in today's shock and awe media environment, it's what generates fear and anger. Negative emotional reactions are three times more likely to lead to clicks and shares. Not only are they finding the most negative and incendiary stories possible, but they are framing them to be even more inflammatory. They'll post ANYTHING that is sure to start a controversy — that includes fake, exaggerated, and engineered news. If it gets clicks, ulterior motives and higher ideals are not considered. This makes watching the mainstream media downright dangerous: not only is it depressing and infuriating by design, but on a long enough time scale and with any faith in the mainstream media, you will be misled and manipulated. They've created an addictive format that degenerates their viewers. It's not sustainable — people burn out, tune out, and check out, or they get desensitized. We stop caring, and in that, we give up the only route to fixing the problems we are watching on the news. By focusing on the problems of the world, we are highlighting the negative. Like a high diver psyching themselves out before the jump, we allow the negativity of the news to prevent us from taking the leap of faith necessary for us to really serve the world at our highest level.

There is also the Werther effect, the copycat syndrome. When a celebrity suicide is spread in the media, copycat suicides follow as well as a rise in fatal accidents of individuals. When the media is sharing stories of mass tragedy, it is wise for a time to avoid public transit, airplanes, and travel in general because of this copycat echo according to Dr. Robert B. Cialdini, psychology professor and author of *Influence: The Psychology of Persuasion*. Those open to negative influence are open to mirroring the action in their own lives — we know the opposite is true too: positive influence leads to positive action.

This is why many high performance experts say: turn the news and mainstream media OFF. High performers skip it entirely. They have no time for it — they are focused on solutions and bold action. If you do find yourself ensnared by negative news or a mainstream (likely manufactured) controversy, counter it with courage and put your energy into action — remember who you are and what your mission is.

What's Holding You Back?

> A miracle is simply something that is impossible from an old story but possible from within a new one. It is an expansion of what is possible.
> ~Charles Eisenstein

It's time for a new story — if we want Unstoppable Enthusiasm, we have to do the work: we have to craft our new story and then begin to live it out. Let's pledge to let go of the past together & set a course for a new future with this book. I'm going to give you the menus and guides to make it happen in your own life, but only you can turn the key and open this door — no one can do it for you. I promise you: if you step into this full force, you will get back the energy you put in magnified; it may take time to develop the mental muscles, but you can and will rewire your brain if you keep at it. Cultivating exponentially greater levels of unstoppable enthusiasm can power you through life's challenges to higher and higher levels of holistic success.

TAKE THE ENTHUSIASM INDICATOR

How much enthusiasm do you have for life?
Take the Assessment & See:
www.matt-powers.mykajabi.com/p/unstoppablereaders

What Held Me Back

While today in certain communities, I stand as a symbol of enthusiasm, positivity, family values, permaculture, and natural living, it was only 16 years ago that I was burning myself with cigarettes, drinking a 6-pack of PBR for breakfast, and staring inwardly at a gaping emptiness. Perhaps it all began with childhood. Though I had a good childhood in some ways, there were also things that happened that took a long time to heal from.

Shortly after starting college, my parents got a divorce. Then at the start of my second year at New York University and while living in downtown Manhattan, the World Trade Centers fell, and the city became a place of military checkpoints, anxiety, fear, and disconnection. I began drinking all day long, smoking cigarettes constantly, and writing songs about the end of the world. I steeped myself in politics, opinions, and judgments. I could argue, intellectualize, and rationalize anything and not care about what we were arguing. I found my way out of anger and fear through disconnection, externalization, and self-righteousness. *They were the problem*, but I was the one with rapidly failing health and waning interest in life.

During my senior year when I got food poisoning from C-Town eggs in Williamsburg, Brooklyn, I almost didn't make it to the hospital. I had been throwing up for too long and had lost too much water. I barely could walk and speak. It was from that point on that digestion was difficult. I'd set off the genes for Crohn's that I'd inherited from my mom's side. It was from that hospital bed that my story began to take a different route. I never again decided to eat white rice and the cheapest eggs for all my meals, so I could spend the rest of my money on Colt 45s.

At the same time, my best friends and bandmates were dabbling in harder drugs, and I was blessed the first time trying heroine with a stark realization that it was poison — that slowing our heart rate, numbing our bodies, and darkening the corridors our minds was playing chicken with death, and I wanted to live. I wanted a life of joy and success. I wanted MORE than a dead end. I already knew how it would go: musician meets drugs; drugs kill musician. The End. I realized that I didn't want to live out someone else's story. I wanted to create my own.

Within a month I was sleeping on friends' couches and in strangers beds, trying to quit cigarettes and spending most of my time on the streets of NYC. I barely attended classes and dislocated from my old social scene, I finally began to feel in touch with life again. As my enthusiasm grew, events, people, and opportunities began to gravitate towards me, and without seeking, I began to find. By embracing the unknown possibility, I began to find the path previously hidden to me. I began to let go of my depression, anxiety, and fears, and that's when I met my wife.

I was sort of dating her roommate, Elna Baker, an NYU student that later would be the New York Times best-selling author and *This American Life* writer, but the moment I saw Adriana, I could hardly be made aware that there was anyone else in the room. It was completely love at first sight.

My first words to my wife were: I know you. You're a punk.

Within days, Adriana and I were orchestrating a group date with my best friend, Andrew, and her roommate, Elna. Andrew wasn't having it and didn't attend, so it ended up the three of us, and then after a few pitchers of margaritas, just Adriana and I.

I think it was the next day that she played *Wouldn't It Be Nice* by the Beach Boys as I entered her apartment that I knew she was my wife with complete certainty. It dawned on me like a joyful epiphany that day. Three weeks later, over margaritas again, I exclaimed that I loved her without realizing that was going to come out... Needless to say, when you are twenty-three years old living in NYC, you don't use that word three weeks into a relationship... but she said *I love you too* and she meant it. It was such a sweet moment of vulnerability, love, and trust.

One morning a few months later, upon waking up next to her, I blurted out in my early morning uninhibited enthusiasm: *Will you marry me?* Smiling, she said *Yes*, and three months later, we were married.

Before we got married, my wife told me she wanted to have the spirit in her life again. I had no idea what she was talking about - *The spirit of fun? Christmas? Huh?* She told me she didn't feel like she could fully explain, and said I should ask her father, Mike, whom I ended up calling. Mike said he'd gotten a prompting a few days prior and had mailed me a book on the subject that should be arriving... that day which of course intrigued me even further.

Now let me explain the context: this was in a time period when Adriana and I were tight on money, she'd quit her job running Stephens-Gabes, a downtown Manhattan flower shop, and she had spent all her savings and her time with me playing shows, traveling, and having fun. Now things were tight, we were working nightclub coat checks and catering together all over the tristate area to pay for our new apartment — drinking and going out became harder to fund. Even before we moved in together and she quit her job, I wasn't able to avoid buying alcohol even when money was tight. She'd ask me to wait for her until after she got back from work to start drinking, but even then I couldn't wait much longer after 11 am. We both had a huge tolerance for alcohol which made it all the more costly. When this book from Mike arrived, I was feeling frustrated with my lack of self-control but wasn't dwelling on it. The book was *Our Search for Happiness*, and it opened my heart to another way of looking at the story of Christ. The next day we attended a fast and testimony meeting at a local church, and I was shocked by the earnestness, the enthusiasm, and the love I witnessed and felt. What was this?? These people, their families, and their behavior were so *nice*. It was during a meeting that day that someone said to me directly: people who drink aren't bad, they are just unhealthy, and in that moment, those words freed me. Their complete confidence that I wasn't bad was so pure that it said YOU ARE GOOD to me, and it was new and preciously sweet for me to feel that confirmation in my heart. I stopped drinking that day and have never been drawn to drinking again. I've learned that even wonderful medicinal tinctures must be held in my mouth until the alcohol is nearly gone before it can touch my stomach, or it will set me back again, killing back the diversity of my delicate gut microbiome.

While my sensitivity to alcohol after drinking so heavily may seem exaggerated, there is more to the story. When my aunt relapsed on alcohol the last time, she passed away at age 52. She and her uncle before her who died at age 35, both fell prey to alcohol and Crohn's disease or nervous stomach as it was called during her uncle's time. Crossing those two wires is a surefire way to destroy our digestion which is the regenerative foundation of our bodies and minds. Many of my friends were convinced I wouldn't live to see 30; I drank so much more than they did and hardly slept. I weighed 139 lbs and was 6'2" when I met my wife.

Marriage, quitting drinking, and John Cusimano's and Rachael Ray's consistent feeding had me at a well-filled in 185 lbs before the move out west though my anxiety and stomach issues were progressively worsening. I wasn't spitting up blood daily any longer, but I was dealing with longer and stronger times of pain. I began to feel my food as it digested, and my wife's cancer came back again. We started digging deeper into alternative cancer therapies and even tried the Gerson Therapy for nearly two years, but I had a bit of nervous breakdown trying to keep it up, and we stopped, hoping that I'd done enough — the 8-12 juices a day plus the special diet plus the full-time job and homeschooling had overwhelmed me. We had cut out meat for the therapy which I didn't mind because I had stopped being able to digest meat without extreme pain. We went vegetarian, then vegan, then raw, but everything felt like a bandaid on a deep wound. I relied upon supplements, essential oils, and herbs to coat the lining of my stomach, to help digest my food, and to numb the pain. For the first few years, I saw doctors, listened, and followed their advice.

It would take many more years of tinkering with supplements, substitutions, different diets, exercise, and meditation to heal myself well enough to wear pants comfortably, but it did happen. New discoveries like Restore, a gut restoration liquid supplement of aqueous humic minerals and amino acid complexes, appeared in my life right as I was given a large quantity of forest-raised pork, rich in incredibly nourishing fats — it was unlike any meat I'd ever eaten before or since. I felt my mouth absorbing the fat even before I could swallow it — between the pork and the Restore, I gained 20 lbs in 6 months and started doing pull-ups for the first time since high school at age 34. It was at this time that I began to hone my daily habits. I'd never been consistent with my yoga or my vocal warmups, but it all changed in 2017.

This is after my first two successful Kickstarter campaigns, after two years of writing *The Permaculture Student 2*, running out of money, losing a tooth, and, at the cost of my health, pushing through the finish line of a 400+ page book. We ran out of money again before we finished shipping the books out. We had to go into overdrive making new sales to pay the new international shipping rates which had risen considerably over the course of writing the book. This was after moving from California to Missouri and back again in the span of 6 months with everything we owned — having no money when we needed to return at the end of that 6 months spurred the launch of two new courses in three months to make it all happen.

I was wrung out. I'd done the impossible. I'd proven I had exuberance, enthusiasm, grit, mastery, creativity, and more, but was I regenerative in my own lifestyle? Was I living sustainably in terms of my energy and the time I spent working? At the end of writing *The Permaculture Student 2*, I was sometimes working 7 am until 2–3 am the next day. My wife and boys would go visit my mom to give me more time without distraction, but that only led to me pushing harder, longer, and, frighteningly, I was losing touch with my enthusiasm trying to stay above water selling and running the programs I'd already started.

On the outside, everyone saw this majestic rise to the top of permaculture education, but from my perspective, I was the only one willing to climb that challenging summit, lose part of myself in the process, and be changed irreversibly by it. I haven't filled in that hole from that tooth — it reminds me of what working too hard can cost me. It reminds me to be careful with my body. I was lucky to only lose a tooth. Many of us can push ourselves past our limits, sometimes without even noticing. Being aware of our sweet spot for high performance takes time and testing, but we have to be looking for it to find it and then learn to hug that turn.

It may seem like an emergency, and it may well be, but we always can take the time to be calmer, more in touch with our breath, and more enthusiastic — which translates to mastery in the moment. Don't let those stresses of the moment pull you away from that perspective — those bills, that fine, that rejection, that failure… *This too shall pass*, and invariably everything always does. Nothing is forever, and the past is a memory that can be let go.

What Have You Overcome?

I bet you've overcome a lot too but haven't shared it with the world. There's no imperative for you to share, but acknowledging what we've faced, if only to ourselves, is incredibly empowering. Additionally, figuring out HOW we overcame those difficulties can be extremely powerful at serving other people and taking our own understanding to another level.

As high performance expert Brendon Burchard says when it comes to finding change in our lives, either something new comes into our lives or something new is generated from within. Sometimes, I would add, it's a combination of the two. For me, it actually was Brendon who came into my life that helped me unlock more of my potential than ever before.

I do not recall how I found Brendon's work, but I found him at a time in my life when I was stuck and looking for a way out. It began with one of his courses, then his book *Motivation Manifesto*, then in a live session of High Performance Monthly Brendon gifted me one of his most powerful programs, *The Experts Academy*, as a way of answering one of my questions. His generosity was astounding to me — I could not have afforded the program at that time. I poured myself into it and studied the contents of the program intensely for months. Using what I learned from Brendon, I launched those two new courses and funded my family's move back to California. We ran out of money again about the time we returned the Uhaul truck. We scraped by in southern California while I planned my most audacious Kickstarter up until that point: *The Advanced Permaculture Student Online*. When we no longer could stay in my late grandmother's home in Orange County, we moved to Washington, outside Seattle, a month before the campaign. In the middle of the launch and despite an ominous bumper-detaching incident as I pulled away, I went out on a speaking tour advertising the new course and selling and signing books from the last Kickstarter's print order. We'd had that truck for less than a year and had barely paid anything back on the loan for it. What started out as a clicking sound escalated to the comical sound made by broken cars on Sesame Street. After the heroic efforts of one of our hosts with a blow torch, my son and I took it in for a professional opinion and learned that we had almost lost a wheel, the bearings were coming apart and about to fail.

Three thousand dollars later, I was ushered by a sheepish and apologetic pair of mechanics to the back of the repair shop. While one of them rocked the truck back in forth for me, so I could hear clinking was still present, the other apologized and explained that they couldn't fix the issue because it was in the transmission and drive train. While it was critical that the ball bearings were replaced, the transmission was clearly too damaged to drive they said. After towing it to a local GMC dealer in American Forks, Utah, we waited days, canceled speaking engagements, and promoted the Kickstarter in a trance. As we went to find out the truck wasn't worth fixing, the Kickstarter nearly concluded at 200% of our original goal!! I went LIVE on Facebook from the dealership parking lot, celebrating both the success and the relief from the financial stress I was facing.

I had to pay off the debt on the truck in full to sell it to the dealership for parts. I then had a choice: continue or go home. I'd already canceled two events. I also had so much stuff: enough to cook our own food, camp, boxes of books, posters, our bags, and a large water dispenser. The cheapest rent was a UHaul from Utah straight home. It felt bittersweet — I'd just had my biggest crowdfunding success yet, but I'd lost a lot of money, my vehicle, momentum on my tour, and a clear idea of what to do next. I was also there with my son at a nice couple's home, so having a pity party would have served no one.

Instead, I did the exact thing I did when my Permaculture Life School Indiegogo campaign failed — I decided to fail upward. I decided to rent a car and drive to San Diego for a few days, and then return to American Fork, Utah, gather our belongings, and then return to Washington. That was one of the best decisions of my life. I decided to go to Brendon Burchard's High Performance Academy LIVE in San Diego instead of driving home immediately.

Now I'm the kind of guy that doesn't react when told to clap your hands together at school. I didn't comply. I didn't conform. I could not lose myself in the moment or be directed by an authority to feel emotionally invested in a group activity, and the more they tried to force me to comply, the more defiant I would get. That was in school, and later as a teacher, I watched students participate in similar group activities with fascination, not understanding. Day two of HPALive, I let go, began to dance, began to jump in place, do Qigong, and take in everything Brendon and his speakers said deeply. In those few days, I let go of the past and I embraced a new concept of myself. I opened myself to a new possibility, to the idea that 2018 would be my best year.

2018: My Best Year Ever

- In 2018, launched my largest course yet, filmed and edited over 150 hours of footage, taught over 500 students, and collaborated with over 60 teachers and over 90 affiliates.
- In 2018, released a new, longer edition of my largest book, 4 translations of my first book, and 3 new books as well as the Permaculture Education Standards.
- In 2018, funded my wife flying to Mexico to film several documentaries-worth of regenerative agriculture footage with her parents.
- In 2018, toured and filmed dozens of sites and interviews across the American West with my son.
- In 2018, shared over $100,000 worth of courses, books, and curriculum
- In late 2018, re-filmed an online course on education and entrepreneurship because I'd learned so much during the year.

By all measures 2018, was my best year, but the tail end of summer, we hit, as a family, a series of health crises. It started with the flu the boys got that didn't go away for weeks. As the boys were getting better, I finally succumbed to the flu, and, for the first time in years, was throwing up. What happened next is something every parent should already know, but I've never heard of: everyone should rinse their mouths out with baking soda and water after they throw up. This counteracts the damaging effects stomach acid has on our teeth. If we just go back to bed, as I did, we run the risk of harming our teeth. If we have Crohn's disease and the inflammation from the flu sets it off, it can take weeks to calm the digestion. I barely ate for weeks and soon had serious pain in my teeth. The dentist later told me it was in part related to my Crohn's but rinsing my mouth with baking soda after throwing up was a critical step I skipped. I had several teeth that were near dead and over a dozen large cavities.

For a short time, I endured the pain, but then it seemed to flare into territory previously unknown to me. I've fractured a knee cap as a teen and skied on it for a week before I gave in, got x-rays, and let it rest. It didn't hurt anything like this. I've broken my wrist, my hand, and toes, but nothing was like the pain of my tooth. Thinking about it actually causes phantom pain — it was so bad.

In fact, returning from a speaking engagement one night, still hours from home, I began to experience unimaginable pain, but I was bound and determined to get home despite the pain. For my son, it was a terrifying experience: I had tears streaming down my face as I wheezed air between my teeth (cold air helped it somewhat), and I was praying incessantly and loudly — perhaps hysterically. I was teetering on the edge of hyperventilation and dizziness, so I kept holding my breath when I'd reach that point to stave off the dizziness. To my son, I must have seemed mad. I don't know how many minutes passed, but at some point, the pain blinked out like a light switch going off. I began to cry tears of joy and gratitude. I didn't stop the breathing pattern, and the pain never came back in full force the rest of the drive home though I could barely walk from the strain on my body when we arrived. My entire frame was stiff and weak. I fell asleep in seconds after collapsing into bed.

This was very much like my college experience with colitis — nearly taken down by illness. My energy, my progress, and more all were sapped. I slowed down with my business, with my body, and with my mind. I became mired in trying to get back on track, further defining myself as off track and, as a result, feeling more and more derailed. We ran out of money again, and Adriana's doctor found more cancer again. It felt like deja-vu. How many times skin cancer? What kind of skin cancer? How bad will the surgery be? And then as we wrapped our minds around treatment protocols for that, the dentist found a mass in her jaw during an x-ray — it was destroying the roots of her teeth and her jaw. The dentist referred her to an oral surgeon and told her it was either a bone cyst or cancer. She came home stressed, and it took time researching, but it became clear: bone cysts don't destroy bone; that's what defines cancer. The oral surgeon's scan would be the first step towards doing a biopsy which is how they verify that it is cancer.

Based on the same principle behind how mammograms spread breast cancer, I knew that breaking the seal made by the body around the cancer would release those cancer cells and spread the cancer — later one of our doctors would agree with this hunch and provide corroborating anecdotal evidence from a former patient of his. I felt a deeper deja-vu at this point; I knew in a moment that if we followed them down that road that I would lose my wife, and she would lose her life. I felt it in my bones and told her what I'd learned and my thoughts on how we had to be very, very aggressive. I told her she MUST change her outlook, she MUST stop complaining, and she MUST meditate every day for hours… Can you imagine how that went over? It didn't work. She didn't even argue or get mad. She deflated in her chair, and tearfully said, *I can see how that is a real solution, but it's like it's just beyond a 20-foot electric fence. It's there, but I can't reach it.* This was devastating for me. I realized that this could be it. This could be the thing that kills my wife, and she saw me crumble which made it even worse for her.

It took days, maybe weeks, of reflection and pressured thoughts to shift into action again. I researched, went public, talked to experts, sought out survivors, and came up with very little. I felt desperate and, in our home, that was mirrored. The dishes didn't get done. Meals were at odd hours. Some days I'd only eat one meal. None of us were sleeping well. After a year of high performance, I was officially off track and so was the entire family. My wife had cancer again except now it was in the bone which was to me, before this time period, a death sentence. The research results also were frustrating — how was my wife to cultivate positivity, enthusiasm, and joy when she felt the opposite? The Youtube video of the stage-IV bone cancer survivor played in my mind again of an ecstatic woman shouting on stage her gratitude and joy. I needed to figure out how to get my wife to start meditating, feeling gratitude, and visualizing her cancer shrinking, so whatever medication or alternative therapy we attempted, it would have the best possible chance of being effective. I needed to figure this out before it was too late — and then as if in response to this exact fear, I heard in my mind: *How is she to feel the joy, enthusiasm, or positivity she needs to heal when you are exuding stress, anxiety, and fear?* This was a breakthrough moment for me. I realized that everything I did from that moment forward was either going to help my wife or hurt her.

I began to pause, look up from my work, and smile a relaxed, warm smile as much as possible whenever anyone, especially my wife, walked into the room. I began to slow down, focusing on my breath, posture, and internal flow of energy. I began to focus on bringing a charged enthusiasm to every moment, every day, and within a couple weeks, things began to change. It became easier and easier to stay in a state of enthusiasm. More sales began to occur. More laughter was heard in our home. We grew closer as a family. We began doing hikes and walks again. We all slept better. We all ate better — I got back on track with dishes and meal times. I began to have new ideas, grand ideas, and Adriana began visualizing the cancer in her jaw shrinking, taking high doses of cannabis and turmeric oils, using cannabis, activated oxygen, and DMSO creams topically, and resting more than 12 hours a day.

Did we change our diet much? Not this time. We're eating everything "wrong": meat, gluten, dairy, and maple syrup — it's all organic and as much as possible regenerative, but we realized it's far better to be joyous, include fermented foods with every meal, take the best supplements possible, and drink probiotic beverages than to stress out over what we are eating in particular. For me, the kitchen is actually the most stressful aspect of my life, so following a path of joy, fermentation, and supplementation is the key for right now. I'm technically highly allergic to nearly everything but meat and seafood because my "leaky gut" allowed all those good foods I was eating into my bloodstream, so my body identified them as invaders. This being the case, I can still eat almost everything if I follow my protocol.

Did she start meditating? Not regularly, but she does try and finds it easy but very tiring. Because she lost her thyroid to cancer over a decade ago, it's hard to predict how everything will work for her. A question I began to ask myself was: *Does she have to do everything?* Does she have to be this machine of protocols? I realized that the most tender places are the most fertile. I realized I could not force her, could not force myself, and could not force the world to change, grow, or heal. I realized I had to allow it to change. I had to let it flow through me. I had to create a still place within me, a tender space, for the healing to begin. After a year of meditation, I'd thought I'd done my introspective work, but I was wrong. I'd only learned to keep the lids on things in my head. I'd never made peace with them. I'd not developed the skills to understand and learn from them. I realized in that moment that I'd been swimming in the shallow end of the pool.

Even meditating 40+ minutes a day, practicing daily yoga, setting my intention, and studying with a high performance coach 1:1, I'd missed the boat… or maybe, as might be the case for you in your life, they were all pieces of a larger progression that didn't make sense until seen in retrospect.

My wife's cancer shrunk 60% in the span of two months while we were waiting for the scan appointment. Was it the visualization? The laughter? The family time? *The cannabis?* Or, was it the feeling that infused them all? Could she have been traveling, taking different protocols, staying with her parents, studying scriptures and praying, and still had the same results? If it was infused with the same level of enthusiastic energy, I'm certain we'd get the same or similar results. Enthusiasm is the vibrant current that runs through all life. When we are in tune with its resonance, we find health, wealth, relationships, and genius flow towards us.

Imagine Yourself...

While it sounds too simple to be true, we are the person we imagine ourselves to be. Close your eyes and imagine that person, see that person, feel that person, and then become that person. This gets easier over time as we practice. It takes real commitment, emotional investment, and patience. Who do you want to be? How would you act? How would you stand and sit? How would you breathe? How would you smile?

The Benefits of Enthusiasm

> Optimism is the faith that leads to achievement.
> Nothing can be done without hope and confidence.
> ~Helen Keller

Feel Good No Matter the Circumstances

Your body hurts all over. It hurts to walk. It hurts to stand up straight. You're broken and beaten. You're behind, and the odds are against you. You waited too long and missed your chance. You made a mistake, and there's no way to fix it. You need to dig deep at times like these, but what exactly are you digging deeply into? *Your Unstoppable Enthusiasm.*

You don't want to leave your house today or even consider conducting a meeting in front of a large group of people, but you know that deep down you want to be the person that does go and serves despite the pain, anxiety, or embarrassment. It is in these moments we decide to become the person we want to be. We could visualize something profoundly joyous from our past to ignite our enthusiasm, or, better yet, we can see our future and emotionally connect to it — if we can step into the emotional state of that memory or projection, we can transcend the pain of that moment. We essentially are tricking our brain by focusing on some of the best thoughts and experiences we've ever had and the body responds to the brain, assuming that is what we are experiencing in real time, and produces the feelings and emotions associated with that memory or projection. This is a game changer: *we can trick our minds.*

When you're facing with your greatest challenges, it's imperative you find your enthusiasm and make it unstoppable! What do you love, what brings you joy, and who do you want to be?

> Enthusiasm is the best protection in any situation.
> ~David Seabury

Joy Amidst the Struggle

Resilience in the face of great adversity is what enthusiasm offers. It's not about being happy or care-free — that's not sustainable and certainly not unstoppable. Joy is transcendent. It can carry us through incredible pain and suffering. With it, we can rise above any situation. Joy can negate or blunt grief, anguish, and despair. It is the precious sweetness that enthusiasm's perspective gives us that can feed our spirits even in the worst of times. It does not erase the pain or the past, but if we can redirect our focus to what connects us with enthusiasm, joy will be ours.

What about the worst days of our lives?

Let's look at the story of Abby Stephens. Paralyzed from the neck down in a car accident, Abby's dreams of marrying and starting her family were abruptly interrupted. She could have said, *Why Me God*? She could have fallen into despair, depression, or anger. She could have blamed her fiancé who was driving at the time, but she didn't. She instead leaned on her faith; she looked within and poured all her focus into her faith. She believed she could be healed by the spirit of God working within her. The first feelings her body initially received were incredibly painful, but in that pain, she felt deep joy knowing that she was healing. Abby's deep religious faith was her enthusiasm, her connection to the divine, and it granted her the joy to push through the pain, visualize the impossible, and make it possible. Against all odds, Abby Stephens went from being a quadriplegic to walking again in only eleven months.

There's a second lesson embedded in Abby's story: she had already developed her deep connection to her enthusiasm before the accident. That is why she was able to bounce back as she did. If we are to be resilient in the face of great adversity, in the midst of pain and terrible loss, we must find our own connection to the divine within us. Everyone's path will be their own, and only you can travel it, but it is worth it. Impossible gifts are waiting for you down that road.

Enthusiasm Keeps Us Focused on the Bigger Goals

When you are enthusiastic, you know exactly why you are that way: you can articulate with great excitement WHY you are deeply grateful and bursting with anticipation. You might have an increased rate of speech, an easy smile that reaches your eyes, or an infectious laugh that draws others to you. You might be prone to tangents or oversharing, but you always return to focusing on your bigger goals. In fact, those conversations primed you somehow — you shared and, in the sharing, increased your enthusiasm and energy. Likely, you have shared more than your new idea or venture, you shared an enlivening jolt of energy. You helped them realize their own passions, goals, and enthusiasm.

Enthusiasm has a watershed effect on our minds. Even as we go off into the thickets, following a new thread of thought, we invariably find ourselves back to the mighty Mississippi of motivation, enthusiasm itself, which swiftly again carries us towards our destination.

Neuroplasticity

To Harness Neuroplasticity, Start With Enthusiasm
~Dr. Helena Popovic

Our brain's ability to adapt and change over time in response to our environment, experience, thoughts, and behavior is called neuroplasticity. It's our innate ability to literally rewire the neural networks of our brain. It can translate to mental flexibility and can grant us adaptability in life's most difficult circumstances. Neuroplasticity is a superpower that can improve everything — including physical performance, but notice the word "harness" Dr. Popovic utilizes; it requires work on our part.

Neuroplasticity can also cause damage — this is something that surprised me in the research but makes sense in retrospect. We can also rewire our brains with *negative neuroplasticity* — negative thoughts, behaviors, experiences, and environments. This is important to note: we are incredibly sensitive creatures — the information we receive from all these aspects of life literally rewires our brains, directly influencing our feelings, relationships, and future experiences. This is why many people try to avoid watching the mainstream news, engaging in pointless social media debates, and arguing with their spouse. Those activities warp our minds. We can do the opposite as well; we can feed our hearts, minds, and bodies an abundance of positivity, creating a resilient and adaptive neural network.

We can rewire our minds with enthusiasm and for enthusiasm.

Life Learning

Enthusiasm naturally leads to life learning. It's the engagement that enthusiasm grants us that powers our continuous learning and growth.

Enthusiasm even allows us to see what opportunities we have even when things are going poorly. It keeps our heads above the tree line and focused on the destination. Transforming our mistakes and tragedies into learning experiences allows us to continually grow and improve, not just over the short term, but for the long haul.

The Son of PA Yeomans, the Australian best-selling author and regenerative farm designer and philosopher, Allan Yeomans has faithfully carried on his father's work, spreading Keyline restoration practices while continuously learning, testing, and expanding upon a myriad of topics in chemistry, geology, flight, farming, soil, and more — all in the context of reversing climate change, restoring soils, and bringing sense to the world. His unstoppable enthusiasm exudes from his writing, his work, and every picture I have seen of him. He is a force of nature. Even at age 88 at the time of writing this, he is showcasing the Carbon Still, a large machine that tests carbon levels in soil samples, so farmers can easily measure their soil carbon levels year to year. If the Carbon Still technology is adopted everywhere, it will allow farmers to finally participate reliably in the still-nascent carbon economy.

At age 85, Allan was still flying in the New South Whales Aerobatic Championships. At 88, he's solving climate change, diving deeper into the chemistry, and leading generations of land stewards forward into the regenerative agricultural era, healing the hydrological systems of the earth while building soils and growing better and better food. If there's a right way to age, Allan has found it deeply rooted in his unstoppable enthusiasm.

When my father was searching for himself again after he and my mother divorced, I encouraged him to play jazz trumpet again. He claimed it had been too long; it had been thirty years since he'd touched the instrument, but I was certain that his enthusiasm for music, for the trumpet, and for excellence would drive him to quickly get back into it. He listened to my advice, bought a nice trumpet, and started playing again. It was revelatory for him and was a pivotal moment in our relationship. He played with a full jazz band orchestra at his wedding only a few years later with his new wife singing alongside him.

Enthusiasm & the Growth Mindset

Carol Dweck's groundbreaking work on the growth mindset, in one concept, captured the difference between those who will and won't succeed. Individuals with the growth mindset believe that they will learn from challenges and difficulties, but those that have a fixed mindset are convinced that they cannot learn from adversity. *Who are these fixed mindset students?* We are anytime we allow those limiting thoughts in such as *I'm not a math person* or *I'm not athletic*. Those are just fixed mindset myths we are feeding ourselves, and, in a very real way, we are just avoiding the difficulty of grappling with them. Carol Dweck's TEDtalk showcases brain scans of children identified as having growth mindsets and fixed mindsets. The scans were opposite of each other — the growth mindset brain scan was red with activity, and the fixed mindset scan was green with inactivity. The fixed mindset students weren't even trying! Saying *I can't* is an immediate bowing out cognitively, so don't do it, and if you do, please insert what Carol has suggested: **YET**. *I can't... YET, but I will some day.*

Enthusiasm is the finest fuel for the growth mindset. With its combination of faith, anticipation, excitement, and gratitude, enthusiasm powers magnificent transformations of all kinds — it quickens, focuses, and directs our learning. It also powers us through the process. Enthusiasm helps us appreciate the journey which is actually the place of real growth, and it's also the place for praise for ourselves and others. Many who achieve great success have found the actual event of being awarded that achievement hollow because it was the challenge that drove them not the status, the money, or awards. Often the satisfaction comes from the growth we experience as we work through our challenges though we need to celebrate our wins, internalize them, and be gracious and honor those that honor us as well.

We are all always in the process of becoming. When we don't believe that, we make it so, and now we have the brain scans to prove it, so honor the struggle, the growth, and the process, and you will always find something to be learned.

Enthusiasm is Contagious

> Nothing is so contagious as enthusiasm.
> ~Samuel Taylor Coleridge

Your conviction is your joy, and others are drawn to it like moths to a flame. Your magnetism is your enthusiasm — it is your pied piper song; sing loud and sing it proud! This is what divides many great teachers from those that struggle for significance in their students' lives. Your students will move mountains if you inspire them, and they will borrow upon your faith and enthusiasm to power them through each challenge. That is the real power of enthusiasm: it's contagious. The students signup without knowing the full story. The customers buy without reading the full description. They try without considering loss if they fail. The authenticity of your enthusiasm builds a bridge of trust they cross with their hearts before their minds consider it.

Because of this, those of us with charismatic enthusiasm, or really any sort of influence over others, are in a powerful position that has very real consequences. We have to be informed, humble, and careful with our enthusiasm because it IS catching — this is why going within and carefully considering what our highest calling is so critical: when we are in pursuit of our highest calling, we are willing to be wrong because it helps us get one step closer to our goal. When we infuse our enthusiasm with humility, we supercharge our ability to learn and grow, and others can recognize when we are in this state. People can see or sense that you are transforming yourself and emanating joy. That energy attracts people — it only comes from joyful learning and growth though, so just being energetic doesn't equate to being unstoppable or contagious: you have to deeply believe in what you are doing or saying.

While I was a young high school teacher in training, I fell in love with seeds. I'd been saving them for a few seasons as a gardener, but from a utilitarian perspective not one of biophilia, the love of nature. When I became enamored with the colors, shapes, sizes, and overall diversity of seeds available for gardeners, it was very interesting to see how many students quickly were interested in saving their own seeds and starting their own gardens. At first they thought it was weird, but after a while, when I didn't tire, when the wonder and inspiration didn't let up, they began to see finally what I was seeing. Many of the best teachers have such powerful magnetism that they can draw children in by their curiosity alone: *What is this woman so enthusiastic about? I want to feel that way too.* Children naturally want to experience and live in enthusiasm — adults too, but we don't allow ourselves to fall in love with the moment as easily. That being said, many an adult will find themselves instantly smiling when encountering a bubbly, giggly baby. An exuberant baby is 100% pure enthusiasm, and that's why their smiles are so contagious.

How can we become more contagious? Become more grateful, present, and ecstatic for what is and what is to come. Enjoy and appreciate the people and world around you to the fullest. Align yourself and your life to that which brings you deepest joy.

Enthusiasm is Attractive

I've had students take my gardening course more for my enthusiasm and what that would do for their lives than for the information in the course. They needed regular high-charge doses of enthusiasm, so they joined my gardening course even though they've been comfortably gardening for decades. They were looking to renew their enthusiasm, not necessarily looking for more skills or information. It took me time to realize this, but this is why students gravitated to my classroom every lunch hour when I was a high school teacher even though I wasn't teaching them anything in particular: they were attracted to the pattern of enthusiasm, not necessarily the content it carried with it. This is why about 30% of all my music classes contained students who had never played music before but were drawn in by my enthusiasm for music, and they wanted to explore that space — especially with me. Many students never shared their music with anyone else but me, and several of the students I worked with one on one, helping craft their vision of a song, are now professional musicians.

Not only is enthusiasm attractive, but it exudes trustworthiness. They can see that you care — it's not about being right or being better than anyone else, you're enthusiastic because you deeply care about the subject and your audience, and they recognize and respect that.

Enthusiasm is Persuasive

Enthusiasm Moves the World.
~Arthur Balfour

With that trust comes the willingness to listen and be persuaded. Enthusiastic people are incredibly persuasive because the listener can't help but associate the enthusiasm they see with the subject being discussed. You weren't ever interested in scuba diving, but after hearing a professional diver describe with eyes-popping and face shining the riot of color below the surface of the Pacific ocean, you are suddenly considering getting your diving certification despite your long-held fear of sharks and open water.

The student that doesn't believe in themselves, takes a chance when that enthusiastic teacher they trust invites them to do so. They may succeed, or they may fail. Often it is how the teacher reacts that carries or corrects the student's initial reaction. Their frustration is malleable to the enthusiastic teacher because of the depth of trust the student feels towards them, but what if you don't have someone in your life who can do this for you?

What if you are the only person in your corner? This is where meditation, prayer, and inner listening come in. We are never alone, and we are never without a counter argument within: whether deeply or superficially, you will find that you disagree with yourself at times. We carry all that we have experienced with us and more — we carry the unknown within us, and this can be the most persuasive at times.

When my wife asked me to pray about moving to California, I did so feeling strongly like it wasn't the time to abandon seven years of hard work and progress in the NYC music scene. I'd developed a fledgling reputation among a few of the top players in the city, and I was working my way into the true inner circuit of professionals. If you study session musicians, you find a pattern of certain players dominating the airwaves, hit songs, and tv appearances, and this inner circle's pattern of passing along gigs to each other is part of the reason why.

I felt pressure, obligation, fear, and stress, but in retrospect, I was starving for meaning as an NYC musician. Climbing the studio musician ladder was the only path before me that I could see myself succeeding at and to quit seemed crazy, foolish, and a slap in the face of so many who had made place for me, advised me, and vouched for me. When she told me she'd prayed and felt like we needed to move, it was like a stone being dropped down the well for me, but I knew I couldn't do anything but pray about it to see if I felt the same confirmation. I prayed and was burned by the answer — quit New York City and leave your dream job along with your entire social network. I struggled with this for a time, but ultimately I knew that it was right, and grudgingly but deliberately I began to disconnect from NYC.

It was in stepping into the unknown, knowing it was right for me, and knowing it was right for my family that opened me again to enthusiasm. It became an adventure, and it was the first real time I trusted an answer from a prayer that I didn't like. That decision opened a door to a deeper enthusiasm: a deeper faith and trust. Since I left NYC, I've done more, experienced more, learned more, and grown more than I ever could have imagined. My success and influence dwarf my time in the NYC limelight despite being on tv to millions and traveling nationally as a touring musician.

> When you put love and enthusiasm into your work, even if people don't see it, they realize that it is there, that you did this with all your body and soul.
> ~Paulo Coelho

Enthusiasm's persuasiveness in many ways is tied to its trust in the unknown — it gives those in your presence trust in you and your vision, even if they don't completely understand why. This is an incredibly sacred thing that must be handled carefully and with reverence. I'm always keenly watching those who are most excited yet least acquainted with my work because they are most apt to misinterpret, misrepresent, and make mistakes. Much like how an enthusiastic toddler will mimic an adult and be surprised by their failure after witnessing the adult easily perform the same task; enthusiasm can lead to people thinking it is easy to do what you are modeling or teaching. Our enthusiasm, support, and guidance will help them overcome the sting of the learning process. If we make a shocked, sad, or scared face to a toddler who finds a difficulty, we will encourage them to emotionally collapse when facing challenges or pain, but if we continue to encourage, enthusiastically and warmly, they try again, overcome the pain, and persevere. All too often the hurt child that is reconnected with their enthusiasm is instantly distracted from pain and irritation. That means their enthusiasm is internally persuading their physical and mental systems to shift focus entirely, and it doesn't have to come from external stimuli: you can generate enthusiasm from within even in the hardest of times. You can form an enthusiastic counterpoint to every negative thought and persuade yourself and others every moment to be better, but it takes consistent intentional habits.

Robert Baden-Powell never intended to create or inspire through his enthusiasm the creation of Girl Scouts and Girl Guides, but that's exactly what it led to. In fact, it was a small group of enthusiastic girls that convinced him through their enthusiasm that girls deserved to and could be excellent scouts. A maelstrom of enthusiasm spiraled outward from Baden-Powell, to a nation of boys and girls, and then on through the world itself, spreading like wildfire. That enthusiasm carried them all forward into the unknown, iterating itself through contagious joy made manifest. In fact, Baden-Powell refused to take credit for the creation of Girl Guides altogether, saying "They started themselves." And I would argue that it is enthusiasm that started it all.

Enthusiasm Brings ENERGY

> Enthusiasm is the steam that drives the engine.
> ~Napoleon Hill

What draws the bee to the flower? Is it the smell, the color, or the taste? Or is it something we cannot see with the naked eye? Recent studies have shown that thermal ENERGY is how bees discern health in flowers. The flowers that release the most energy are the most attractive. People, too, are attracted to energy, exuberance, and enthusiasm. Enthusiasm's energy is extremely powerful because it is self-sustaining — the energy leads to specific actions that feed the roots of their enthusiasm, maintaining and generating more energy and enthusiasm. The wins, or even the promise of a win, are enough to sustain the enthusiastic through setbacks. Turning their failures into learning experiences, they feed them into the fire and keep moving forward. Others also feed off that energy and mirror it back — this is what happens during a powerful performance. This is the musician on stage putting everything they have into the music: the audience mirrors their energy both through their engagement and response between and sometimes during the songs. The intensity of their applause or engagement is correlated to the energy the musician is putting out. This is not to say the louder or more frenzied gain more followers — authenticity is the hallmark of true enthusiasm: the songs may be loud, quiet, slow, or fast. It is the enthusiasm the person puts into it that we are really witnessing and lending our own energies to.

Enthusiastic energy is what propels our greatest leaders. This is the energy that powers entrepreneurs on little sleep and stacked odds. This is the energy the athlete relies upon to give them the edge and to keep them in the zone. This energy is what powered Theodore Roosevelt, Fred Rogers, Richard Simmons, Amelia Earhart, and PT Barnum, and what powers Oprah, Ellen DeGeneres, Desmond Tutu, Ed Mylett, and Brendon Burchard. They are connecting to their enthusiasm to generate their energy.

Greatness for each of us is individual, but for all of us, it is deeply rooted in our enthusiasm.

The lowest energy time periods in my life have also been my most depressed, and inversely, the days of my greatest success have always been infused with an almost electric charge of enthusiasm. This is no accident. We sometimes wake in this state — we feel AMAZING and are excited for the day. Learning how to generate this state, and not encounter it by luck, is what this book is ultimately about. We can train our minds and bodies to expect and generate the feelings and thoughts we want to have.

Enthusiasm Opens Hearts... & Doors

> Success is the ability to go from failure to failure without losing your enthusiasm.
> ~Winston Churchill

Enthusiasm's energy comes from connecting to our heart, to our deepest personal truths. We speak and act from the heart, and people take notice. When groups of people regularly sing, chant, and, I suspect, dance together, their heart rates begin to synchronize. Studies have shown this be true for at least the singing and chanting — these are often our most exuberant forms of human expression. Enthusiasm speaks to us from the heart and unites our hearts as one. This is why inauthentic enthusiasm is so offensive, because they are trying to fake heart communication, and we can sense the difference.

Heartmath Institute's research has shown that every part of the body generates an electric field and that the human heart creates the largest field reaching outward in a six to ten-foot radius. Our hearts are powerfully communicating to the world around us, and they do not lie. This is why people can sense true intent, even without direct proof. This is also where intuition is found — it's been proven through HeartMath's research that the heart knows before the brain what is going to happen next. Our intuition, our gut reaction, actually comes from our heart, and when we communicate from the heart, we essentially speak heart to heart, skipping the rationale mind altogether.

While I often get credited with being enthusiastic, I pale in comparison to my children's abilities in this area. Often their enthusiasm and excitement lead people to give them things. Our oldest has come home with switchblades, scholarships of all sorts, nice clothes, autographed books, surfboards, wetsuits, rock climbing gear, and more — people just want to give him things, talk with him, and soak up his dazzling energy. While that may seem like receiving gifts are a nice perk of being enthusiastic, it's indicative of something much deeper: all these gifts were gifts in return. They weren't given in a vacuum but out of reciprocity for the gift my sons' enthusiasm gave to those people.

Enthusiasm melts the unlikeliest hearts as well — our youngest will walk up to the roughest, gruffest, aloof, or even angriest looking or seeming people and disarm them, surprise them, and flip their day within moments. His earnest joy and enthusiasm reconnect these folks feeling lost with what makes them enthusiastic, and they end up sharing their private passions, hopes, and dreams with our little inquisitive Oliver. By seeing through their rough exteriors, he lets them reach their own interiors again. Enthusiasm unlocks hearts rusted shut and brings light where there is darkness inside our minds. It also allows us to see people for who they truly are.

Enthusiasm Connects Us All

> If you have zest and enthusiasm, you attract zest and enthusiasm. Life does give back in kind.
> ~Norman Vincent Peale

Enthusiasm has the power to spread virally and erase boundaries of separation even as it gets us in touch with our individual personal passions. Your excitement reminds me of my excitement, and in an atmosphere of open sharing and celebration of each other's passion, we find the kinship within all human beings for each other and for the shared spirit of enthusiasm itself.

Research shows that emotions of all kinds are able to spread within a group. While this could have been misleading at times, early humans were likely more often rewarded for mirroring fear, joy, courage, and wonder as a group. Catching emotional states virally unified our ancestors as a group which made them more resilient and responsive to the environments in which they found themselves. Today, enthusiasm has the potential to guide our communities, families, and lives towards their greatest expressions. We can spread the emotional states we want to see in the world by embodying them openly and letting others witness it.

A Clarity Exercise:

- *Write down all the ways you want to feel and things you want to experience*
- *Visualize each experience and feeling with and without enthusiasm*
- *Enthusiasm is the thing that creates desire. This begs the question: Is it that thing or feeling we desire or is it enthusiasm we are really needing?*

If we remove our enthusiasm and we no longer have a passionate connection to someone or something we love, what does that mean? It's time to get below Enthusiasm's surface and see what's going on under the hood.

Imagine Yourself...

Imagine yourself infused with the electric charge of unstoppable enthusiasm. Imagine what you can accomplish. What dreams are waiting to be realized? What new frontier would you explore? You have boundless energy! You feel light on your feet but powerful, like a dancer preparing to leap. Time seems slowed down, somehow sweeter. Colors are brighter, and you feel like you can do anything. You are living in enthusiasm!

The Roots of Enthusiasm

Enthusiasm is a brilliant mix of gratitude, anticipation, faith, and excitement. This cocktail supports and fosters an entire family of beneficial states: our confidence, focus, clarity, connection, proactive energy, and more. If we want to taste the best fruit from the tree of life, we need to nourish the roots of our enthusiasm and stay deeply connected.

Gratitude

> Gratitude is not only the greatest of virtues, but the parent of all others.
> ~Marcus Tullius Cicero

Being grateful is immeasurably powerful. Expressing sincere gratitude creates a bond in time that is both pure and purifying. Think about a time when you were genuinely thankful to your core — what happens to your chest, neck, and face? There's a lift; we are filled with that gratitude, and we feel and can even appear radiant. Under gratitude's guidance, we are transformed and, in turn, so too, the world around us. New doors appear and open, new insights leap out of the woodwork, and new people come into our lives. We become a magnet for more to be grateful for.

When we are grateful, we are more open and even child-like in our wonder and curiosity though it doesn't mean we are blind or naive. We are also more relaxed internally when we express or feel gratitude, even as we are more aware of the moment. Gratitude highlights the possible and the positive, and from that vantage point, we can spot wisdom and solutions more easily.

The moment I awake and rise from my bed each morning, I say quietly to myself as not to disturb my wife and two sons: *Thank you, Thank you, Thank you, Thank you...* in a quieter version of the late Wayne Dyer's waking mantra. I then go to my office to continue my morning routine which has gratitude woven throughout it.

Embedded in my morning affirmations is a section dedicated solely to gratitude:

Thank you for:

Thank you for: my life, my body, my mind, my heart, my friends, my family, my wife, my children, my home, my success, my failures, my lessons learned, my growth, my routine, my strength, my clarity, my trailblazing, my lynchpinnery, the Spirit that runs through all life and all things, the examples I've had in my life of greatness, honesty, kindness, and love.

I am so blessed. I am so grateful to be given this opportunity. I won't waste it.

These are my morning gratitudes — we all can write our own. We can read them aloud each morning and throughout our day, generating gratitude within ourselves. These can work as a powerful reset when we get off track. Keeping a gratitude journal is a reflective activity that frames our days in gratitude before bed, releasing the negativity of that day and focusing our minds on positivity, so we wake the next day expecting good things. If we go to bed stressed enough times in a row, we begin to wake stressed. Similar to how bad news or shocking images drive all thought from our minds, gratitude has that same effect. It can cancel out fear and pain and bring us back to our best selves.

Gratitude frees us from emotional pain.
~Jane Ransom

Gratitude for being in the present moment and gratitude for our breath, both connect us to the moment in a way that feeds our enthusiasm without relying on any outside stimulation. I am grateful to be here. I'm thankful to be alive. I am thankful for this breathe. I am grateful for my body. It is a joy to be here and to be alive. Taking time to revel in this simple gratitude is critical to developing unstoppable enthusiasm.

Anticipation

It's Christmas Eve; you're a little kid and can't wait for Santa. The feelings of anticipation are almost electric — you can't sleep, you're giddy, and your mind is teeming with creative thoughts as you imagine tomorrow's potential gifts. *Will it be this? This? That? Or THAT? Or… Those.* The energy and creativity of anticipation supercharges our mind and body. Young courting couples go to great lengths and expense to be elaborately clever with their invites, dates, and proposals. We will do almost anything for that special someone in anticipation of a deeper level of relationship with them.

> *Wisdom consists of the anticipation of consequences.*
> ~Norman Cousins

Anticipation can also be seen as simply the expectation of something. We might anticipate a ball hitting our head and instead duck out of the way, but this, too, is relevant. The effect of being able to prepare for, predict, and respond adaptively to the future is in direct relation to the energy, intention, and attention we pour into the current moment where life is unfolding into the future in real-time. Anticipation is also related to gratitude: it's gratitude for something that hasn't happened yet.

Faith

> Enthusiasm is faith set on fire.
> ~George Adams

Enthusiasm at its most literal is *En Theos* or *In God*, so faith is a key component to its practice. To be divinely inspired, to allow the spirit of God to enter us, to activate or unlock our own divine nature is fundamental to enthusiasm. It's important to note, faith and enthusiasm are not claimed by any one religion, science, or philosophy but recognized, studied, and honored by all. Faith is the belief and trust in things unseen or unrealized. When we have authentic faith, we let go of stressing over the unknowns in our lives and, instead, are filled with gratitude for what is and what can be — and the relief that comes from this is profound and very real. We are both emotionally connected and validated by faith — whether it be in a church, on top of a mountain, or in our hearts: it is real and deeply nourishing for each individual to believe good things are coming and that we live in a benevolent universe that wants us to succeed. It may have a name for you, it may involve others, or it may be intensely private and nameless, but it's the same for us all: we thrive when we have faith in ourselves, in each other, and in the world we live in.

Growing up, I never had to be convinced into believing in an unseen force, spirit, or god though that wasn't a priority in my household. I simply had a series of close calls growing up where I nearly died. Serious car crashes where I came out of my seatbelt and hit the windshield but suffered not a scratch. Skiing accidents where I hit and broke the brand-new pads covering snowmaking piping that were installed the day before I hit them — I was going ~50 mph and not wearing a helmet. Or the time I fell asleep on the highway, waking as I dipped the nose of my Jeep between the tractor trailer's back wheels. There were times I listened to my gut, walked away, didn't go down that alley, and sometimes then watched my instincts confirmed moments later. I have faith that I'm being watched over, protected, and guided when I need it most, and I find that it invariably is the case that I am protected and guided. Is it luck or is it faith?

But is faith just wishful thinking? Delusion? Irrational? Actually, more and more scientific proof from research and studies in quantum physics suggest Buddhism, Christianity, Judaism, Taoism, and more were on to something. Faith is the key to creativity, growth, healing, and mastery. Faith is how we draw those desirables into reality.

Enthusiasm in many ways is God in us or at least our connection to the divine — if we are rooted in that feeling we can love people more completely than in any other state. If we have a desire to change someone or to help someone find change in their lives, changing ourselves is the key. Show them that you are immovable, unshakeable, and growing consistently in your faith and enthusiasm. This, I've only recently come to recognize, is one of the main reasons I love and cherish my wife — when we are together and things are aligned, I can access the highest levels of my enthusiasm, and *surprise, surprise*, she ends up mirroring that exact state: my enthusiasm helps her unlock her own, and, in turn, her enthusiasm brings me even more joy.

Of course, the opposite is true: my negative emotions are just as easily spread. I've realized that rather than mirroring the emotions of our partners when they are in a bad mood or stressed, we need to stay connected to our enthusiasm in such a way that their judgments, emotions, doubts, and negative thoughts don't affect us, and instead we bring them over to our energy. We can defuse the tension, help find the solution, listen, or just show them we care and we're there for them. Only when we are connected in that way can we show them love and faith that transcends that moment.

Others can borrow upon our faith — they can trust our trust in the unseen and unrealized, but it's not a strong connection, and over time it will be tested and can fail. Learning to cultivate our faith is similar and just as personal as cultivating our enthusiasm. It takes time, but in that process, faith also creates patience because there is a trust that it will happen. This patience sustains us in lean times. We have faith that it will get better and that we are enough.

Faith & Self Confidence

> Whether you think you can,
> or you think you can't — you're right.
> ~Henry Ford

You have to have faith in yourself to do anything. Just as you have to have faith in others to work well in a team or a marriage, we all exist on the faith that we can see a positive outcome for ourselves and others. Having faith in ourselves is believing that we have the potential for greatness and already possess intrinsic worth. We can see ourselves gaining the skills and understanding we need to be successful. It is this initial boost of confidence that begins the confidence-competence loop, but it all starts with the faith that you can learn and grow. As you progress, you develop your competence and gain in confidence which is a deepening of your faith in yourself. Confidence is vital for us to have faith that we can accomplish our dreams. That means that enthusiasm includes faith and self-confidence as well as gratitude and anticipation.

Meaning & Purpose

What gives us meaning and purpose in our lives? I would argue simply that both are tied to our enthusiasm. If we can tease that thread out, we can follow it all the way into our heart of hearts. It may seem a bit like *Which came first, the chicken or the egg?* but without each of the components of enthusiasm, we would not feel connected to our purpose and we would not find meaning in our lives and work. It is enthusiasm, infusing our day with the radiance of being connected to the divine within us that gives us purpose and creates meaning in our lives.

Community Harmony & Evolution

Detailed in *Exuberance: The Passion for Life*, exuberance must be witnessed and shared with others to be considered such. I believe something similar is true with enthusiasm. It cannot help but be shared even though we can cultivate it privately — it is a thing we witness in others and in ourselves. We don't end up with secret enthusiasms — instead, these things we RADIATE, and people can sense and see it. Enthusiasm has the ability to communicate excitement, inspiration, faith, gratitude, and anticipation without words — this may be why it is such an ancient human modality. It transcends language barriers, disarms, connects, unites, entertains, educates, and intrigues. Enthusiasm courses through every strong family and community.

It is also the primary modality of children and babies: they are enthusiastic beings by nature, full of spark and energy! Their enthusiasm engenders a genuine affection that brings out the best in their caretakers, community, and themselves. If we want to heal our communities and strengthen our families, we need to bring more enthusiasm to those areas.

Imagine Yourself…

Imagine yourself feeling more gratitude, having more faith, feeling more anticipation, and, overall, having more excitement in your life. What are you doing? How are you feeling? What ideas are you having? What connections are you making?

The Daily Habits of Enthusiasm

> No one keeps his enthusiasm automatically.
> Enthusiasm must be nourished with new actions,
> new aspirations, new efforts, new vision.
> ~Papyrus

There are many and even some unique ways to amplify and reignite our enthusiasm, but I'm going to start with the most powerful and actionable first: the morning and evening rituals. During the day when we are working and caught up in the chaos, we may not be able to remember all the other habits, but the resetting at night and priming each morning will make a profound change in your life within weeks if not days.

Enthusiasm is INDIVIDUAL and, at times, eccentric. You may find yourself having a very different morning ritual from others or a consistently fresh combination of morning rituals that form a unique rhythm for you — this is why I created a menu for both morning and evening rituals. All too often we have exact instructions from a guru on how to start our morning without any choice on our part. We just have to stick to the program, or we fear that we could jeopardize our progress. When we fail to keep up the strict regiment set out in their latest book, we tend to feel like we've failed. We might even feel guilty like we've let them down, but from all my research, I can tell you that there is not a single universal formula for successful morning routines: not everyone who is successful meditates, not everyone successful does yoga, not everyone successful can run, and so on. The commonality is all these practices serve to reset and prime our minds. I've been exploring, researching, and testing morning routines from a broad spectrum of individuals past and present. If we can master this practice of resetting and priming, no matter the exact expression, we will have control over our days, our tempo, and our outlooks.

I must confess: some mornings I cannot move energetically or focus in those first 10–20 minutes of the day. This is primarily a product of pushing myself too hard, but on those days, I rely upon meditation, affirmations, breathing, and priming myself with powerful videos, audio, reading, and memories that I visualize. Sometimes I can't speak, my throat is too sore, but I mouth the words as if I can, knowing that to my brain I'd still be speaking them. Later, usually after working out, when my body is more oxygenated and open, I often use the Roger Love daily vocal warmup to reverse the effects of the sore throat, headache, or head cold.

Would you rather push through feeling miserable or would you like to wait for the moment when obstacles will lighten and evaporate? If we do the work, finding our enthusiasm can flip our situations in an instant.

> Enthusiasm is the electricity of life. How do you get it? You act enthusiastic until you make it a habit.
> ~Gordon Parks

It's important to differentiate enthusiasm from exuberance. There is a fixed mindset thread in the scientific studies of exuberance which is often, even by the scientists themselves, considered interchangeable with enthusiasm, though it is not. Enthusiasm can become a habit while exuberance is categorically closer to ecstasy and mania and is related to higher levels of energy typically from birth. If you read *Exuberance*, the repeated message is that genius is related to exuberance, and these individuals are born that way. It's, in part, anathema to the more recent and broadly researched insights into neuroplasticity, meditation, and the growth mindset. We can change, we can rewire, and we can grow into new people even if we are lower energy, have disabilities, had a challenging childhood, or feel lost right now. Humanity's ability to learn to exude a joy for life is not limited to special people or some inner circle of university professors — you can find your enthusiasm, make it a habit, and hone it until you are UNSTOPPABLE!

Each must look within for those parts of themselves that connect to the unstoppable: love, gratitude, awe, wonder, curiosity, care, joy, peace, and oneness. While each path is unique, the steps are the same.

Reaction vs Intention

What kind of day do you look forward to?

Another email, another text, another Facebook update, another headline scandal, another friend request, and so on — we are faced with unlimited stimuli, but what is that doing to us? Are you feeling overwhelmed? Micromanaged? Having to be always "On"? Or maybe you're always trying to please others or answer their requests? Are you constantly feeling exhausted by it all, wanting to catch up only to find it all back again the next day? Enough is enough — take back your life TODAY. Turn OFF the cellphone, delete those apps, turn off notifications on your phone, and don't check your email until afternoon. Set aside time to react and then when the time is up, end it, and get back to setting your intention, to creating your day and your life.

Setting our intentions is the key to accomplishing anything great in our day — if we are caught in reaction, we will never achieve our highest goals. Set the course for your day, and you will be rewarded with more and more enthusiasm as you achieve, learn, and grow.

The Morning Ritual

Once upon a time, my morning ritual was a six-pack and sorrow - I'd wake up and count my misfortunes. For many people, the first hour (and the last) are the most lonesome, dark, and dangerous. Today I wake up, drink 8–12 ounces of water, and joyously count my blessings — though affirmations and gratitudes are just one component of my routine. Many of my morning rituals expand, so if I'm not feeling it that morning, I can add in more or take it slow depending on what's off. Sometimes my back or shoulder prevent yoga, but then I focus more on doing extra breathing exercises. Some days my body is so alive that I continue working out well past yoga: doing pull-ups, physical therapy, jogs, and sprints. Some days I forget to do my vocal warmups, but if I'm filming, I usually always do a warmup prior. Every day is its own.

I want every reader and reading to feel open to interpretive growth. I don't want to give a rote set of behaviors and techniques because what we can or choose to do differs for everyone at different times in our lives. It's far more important to understand the purpose of these morning rituals, so we can always achieve them, no matter the configuration of our morning. We all want to start our day feeling renewed and joyously enthusiastic for the day.

Things to Avoid in the 1st hour of the day
- Your Cell Phone
- Social Media
- The News
- Screens
- Negativity
- Eating

Affirmations

Have you heard of affirmations already and felt like they wouldn't work for you? There are some caveats here that are critical. Some have said that saying affirmations that we don't believe or feel has no benefit. This seems similar to the idea circulating that our brains don't hear negation: instead of hearing I will not eat that type of food any longer, the subconscious supposedly hears: I will eat that type of food. While it is true you don't want to fixate on the things you wish to avoid, these popular generalizations are contrary to the research and results of Marisa Peer, who is considered to be the #1 therapist in Britain. Through her work, she has come to realize that the body IS the subconscious mind, and it responds to everything we say, and while it understands negation, it does not understand sarcasm or exaggeration. In other words, when you say: *My job is killing me.* Your body hears that and believes it. From that moment forward, your body's mission is to prevent you from going to work. You might develop a medical condition, depression, anxiety, and more — all to save you from going to work. Marisa Peer, in a very short period of time using affirmations, her personal brand of therapy, and a mild form of hypnosis can reset and reprogram the mind and body. This is very similar to Dr. Joe Dispenza's meditation program where one meditates for 20 minutes and then practices visualizing affirmations and emotionally connecting to those affirmations. From this perspective, affirmations and meditative states are incredibly powerful tools that we can utilize in a variety of contexts to reset and prime our minds and bodies.

These reprogramming events are happening when we are deeply relaxed but not asleep — you are aware and remember it all. This is why it is best to do affirmations of any kind first thing in the morning and just before bed when we are naturally relaxed and mentally open to suggestion. Writing out our own affirmations at this time of day can be very powerful, and since they are written in that twilight state, it is very natural to accept and resonate with the words you've written. They fundamentally are true to you because they are generated from you. If something doesn't resonate with your higher self, your inner wisdom, it IS rejected and you may even pull out of the relaxed state which helps us recognize when it is happening. As you focus on going deeper into these meditative states, you will be able to increasingly ignore, deflect, and dissolve anything that doesn't resonate with your inner truth.

Does that mean I can't listen to or borrow other people's affirmations?
Not at all! I'll include my own, so you can get an idea of what you can start out with. I love variety, so I'm always checking out the affirmations that people share, and I'm always editing and adding to my own affirmations in reaction. Feel free to start with my affirmations, or write out your own, and adapt from there.

Are affirmations only for after we wake and before we go to sleep?
No — you can repeat them throughout your day, have an afternoon meditation/affirmation session, or post them on the walls and over doorways in your workspace and home.

Our affirmations can also have triggers. I use a mirror trigger for a very special affirmation set: *I love you, I am proud of you, You are enough.* It's short, but it's a powerful reminder and feeds me emotionally. Much of Marisa Peers work is around addressing the widespread feeling that folks feel they are not enough. I find this particular affirmation set and trigger very powerful. For many who feel like a parent didn't say *I'm proud of you* or *I love you* enough, this is an opportunity to fill that tank.

Affirmations are simply statements that we solemnly declare — they affirm what we believe or would like to believe to be true. This is incredibly powerful because our subconscious minds, our bodies, hear the statements as true, and then try to live in accordance with that truth. We are also preparing our minds to experience that reality. This translates into confidence and deep enthusiasm later on when sharing your ideas or when truly experiencing their fruition in real-time.

When we start our day with affirmations, we invoke gratitude and push out the pain, the irritation, and the fog. *WE REMEMBER WHO WE ARE.* We reconnect with the person we want to be every morning and get to start our day on our own terms.

I AM Affirmations

I am unstoppable

I am Enthusiasm

I am POWER

I am Wealth

I am MORE THAN ENOUGH

I am Peaceful

I am Balanced

I am Grateful

I am FREE

I am Happy

I am Loved

I am Loving

I am the BEST

I am the Greatest

I am the Lynchpin

I am the Trailblazer

I am the Exemplar

I am God

I am Spirit

I am Energy

I am Light

I am Truth

I am All Possibilities

I am Courageous

I am Wise

I am Kind

I am Compassionate

I am Masterful

I am One with All Around Me

I am a best selling author

I am a billionaire

I am…

Download & Print It Out:
www.matt-powers.mykajabi.com/p/unstoppablereaders

At first, you might find yourself not "feeling" it. This is the real struggle — it's all words if we don't actually feel different. How do we get past borrowing other's enthusiasm to start generating our own? It takes getting in touch with ourselves; it takes knowing what brings us gratitude, and that takes time.

You also might find my affirmations don't fit your situation or ambitions, and that's exactly why I encourage everyone to create their own. You might have a knee jerk reaction to 'I am God'; it's there to remind me to live in complete alignment with God such that we are one. You might say "I am Everything", "I am Love" or "I am Light" — they are words that describe something beyond words. The "I am a billionaire" might also strike some nerves, but I'm convinced if someone generates billions from regenerating the earth and spreading joy and empowerment, they are using their funds wisely and generating positive, holistic change in the world, and we need that now more than ever. We need massive change, and that is what I'm visualizing with that affirmation: I'm seeing the forests replanted, the bison herds return, the oceans restored, the deserts regreened, girls educated, and starving folks fed because that is what being a billionaire means to me. I hesitated to share both of these but did precisely because they are so personal. You likely will have similar affirmations that you, too, will be hesitant to share. They might not make sense taken out of context from your morning affirmations and your personal perspective, but they often will be rich with meaning and have the ability to connect us deeply to our enthusiasm.

Gratitudes

Expressing gratitude the moment we awake connects us from the fog of sleep to our best selves in moments. Just saying *Thank You* has this effect. While I quietly or silently say this mantra as I leave the bedroom, I elaborate on my gratitude with my morning affirmations, specific gratitudes, and positive projections. Below is the paragraph of gratitude I read every morning in the first 5–10 minutes of my day.

Thank You For:

Thank you for: my life, my body, my mind, my heart, my friends, my family, my wife, my children, my home, my success, my failures, my lessons learned, my growth, my routine, my strength, my clarity, my trailblazing, my lynchpinnery, the Spirit that runs through all life and all things, the examples I've had in my life of greatness, honesty, kindness, and love.

I am so blessed. I am so grateful to be given this opportunity. I won't waste it.

This is included in the Affirmations Download:
www.matt-powers.mykajabi.com/p/unstoppablereaders

I also, at the end here, acknowledge my blessings, reaffirm my gratitude for those blessings, and then commit to honoring those blessings. Blessings are just things we are grateful for in our lives. When we count our blessings, we can become more aware of ourselves, our circumstances, and the true possibilities available to us. We let go of negative emotions. We reset, popping up like a buoy momentarily held beneath the waves.

Positive Projections

When we set a goal, we are casting a positive projection out into the unknown future. This is where all possibility begins. Unfortunately for many, negative projections have the same ability to find their way into our lives. When we say we can't, we can't. When we say we can, we open up the door to a new possibility. If you are fixated on the worst case scenario and not the best case scenario, you are never going to end up with the best results.

Once we've reset ourselves and let go of limiting feelings and thoughts, now is the time to prime — we set our intentions for what we want to see, feel, and experience in our day. There's some overlap between the I AM section for sure, but I also included that too, so you could feel free to flow in all directions with your affirmations, projections, and gratitudes. You can even combine all three concepts in one statement: *I am so grateful for the gifts this day will bring.*

Positive projections only have power if we are feeling emotionally connected to them. Only when we can feel what it is like, do we prepare our minds and bodies properly for that reality to come true. This is vital — if you are repeating a mantra while feeling disconnected, you are saturating those statements with that disconnection. This can be very deep work once we recognize how sensitive and influenceable we are as beings. We are influenced and can influence ourselves and each other to the core quite easily, but we also can use this modality to build resilience and strength, so that, eventually, we are immune to those undesirable influences. This requires creating strong associations with these projections prior to encountering outside influences — this is why cell phones and social media do not mix with a powerful morning routine.

The following are my personal positive projections, so they may not be exactly what works for you. That's okay; in fact, it's excellent because it means you have your own vision to share, maybe different wording or a different focus, but it's yours, it's strong, and it's there waiting for you. I beg you to go and find it because no one can find it for you, and this life is about finding paths of purpose and meaning.

I Will

I will not be slowed down by those afraid to try.

This is my day - I will make it great.

I will see the Child of God in those I meet today.

I will choose what is right even when it is hard.

I will honor the journey.

I will show love, patience, and kindness.

I will grow with nature, knowing that I too am always changing and learning.

I will meet those I encounter in my day with all the warmth and presence I can.

I will make time for time.

I will be debt free.

I will be free of doubt.

I will be a NY times & Amazon best selling author.

I will give myself the freedom to be my best self, to make mistakes, and to do better the next time.

I Am

I am healthier than I've ever been.

I am resilient in the face of great adversity.

I am uncompromising with my values and beliefs.

I will honor those that I disagree with even as I disagree with them.

I've put in my time. I've come so far. I'm ecstatic to be here right now.

I trust myself. I trust that I will know what to do. Something great will happen.

Today

Today will be the greatest day of my life - I don't know how or why yet, but I'm ready for it. Ready for it to be joyous.

Today I will find a deeper connection with those I love.

Today I will bring my best self to every moment.

Today I will continue my good habits and leave behind any bad habits.

Today will be the start of something new.

Download & Print It Out:
www.matt-powers.mykajabi.com/p/unstoppablereaders

Meditation & Prayer

Studies on the positive benefits of meditation have been amassing exponentially, showcasing a broad spectrum of benefits. Studies have uncovered how meditation moderates cortisol levels, providing more resilience in times of stress. Controlling pain and even lowering blood pressure can also be accomplished through meditation.

But what is meditation and how does it differ from prayer?

Often meditation is referred to as mindfulness or just focusing on one's breath. Mindfulness is a deep, relaxed state of awareness of the moment in real-time. Being present is another way of describing it. When we focus on our breathing, we naturally become relaxed, but it's more than that: we can change our brain waves from a beta to an alpha state. When we fall asleep, we travel through our brain wave states until we are in a delta wave state — usually referred to as deep sleep. In the morning, we move from delta to theta to alpha to beta again, but since we were just in alpha, when we meditate in the first hour of the morning, we can very easily slip back into that state. Some meditate immediately upon waking. Some pray. Some do Qigong, yoga, or run trails in a meditative way. They are all reaching for the same place: a deeper state where the mind is calm, our connection to our enthusiasm is complete, and our vision is clear. You may find yourself crying when in this state. I certainly do. I cannot recall a morning without tears in recent times. The writing of this book has been primarily done in a meditative state and often with tears in my eyes. I believe our greatest art and expressions await us in our meditative states. Beauty comes to us pure and untamed, and we weep, overwhelmed with the joy of it, the joy of being alive in this moment.

A prayer is an act of faith — we're pouring our gratitudes, needs, fears, hopes, and desires into the hands of God, into the unknown. We are putting down the weight of our worries and leaning upon faith instead. We believe in ourselves, in others, and the world we live in that good things are waiting for us all and that we all are enough to love and be loved. We can say a prayer during meditation or in prayer meditate upon the words we hear or are studying. The practices and their overlap are beautifully diverse in how they can be applied universally and individually.

How Much Meditation?

At least once a day for at least 20 minutes. Some will say at least 5 or 10 minutes but ideally 20. I find that I don't "let go" until 12-15 minutes in, so 2–5 minutes is fine for transitioning between activities during our day, but for starting our day, I would always lean towards 20 minutes as a minimum. That is the minimum length of time most studies have found to be associated with the most benefit. I try to do 40 minutes in the morning, but I have a goal to do another 40 minutes in the afternoon.

What kind of Meditation?

There are many types of meditation, and they all have unique advantages and effects. I have been practicing meditation for only 2 years, but it is a daily practice which in many ways determines the course of my day. When I started out, I'd sometimes miss a day here and there, and my wife would usually be able to tell within seconds if I had forgotten to meditate — without meditation, I was more easily distracted, frazzled, and irritated. As I've spent more time trying out different meditations, I have come to realize that I've been using meditative states in songwriting, performance, and competition since I was a very young child.

I have also figured out that if I'm too restless for my usual 40-minute meditation that I can do simpler 20-minute meditation. The point is we get to take a break from trying so hard, from being something, from being who were, or who we want to be — it's liberating to just let things flow in and out of us without holding onto them or reacting to them. This blank space within us that only meditative states create is the ultimate reset button. Having a hard day? Meditate. In pain? Meditate. Feeling down or hurt? Meditate. Got writer's block or looking for that next big inspiration? Meditate.

Is meditation a cure-all?
No, but it has a broad spectrum of benefits that mitigate so many stressors. Meditation and certain breathing techniques, like the Wim Hof method, can have superhuman effects — some of which I can share from personal experience.

Types of Meditation

Seated, Standing, Walking, & Lying Down - While these may describe the main accepted physical modalities for meditative states, I would add that the "zone" of performance and competition can also be a meditative state.

Focused Attention - This is simply concentrating on a single focus for an entire meditation session. There are many types of concentration meditations such as focusing on one's breath, focusing on a flame, or focusing on an external fixed point or object.

Open Monitoring or Mindfulness - This type of meditation is characterized by being present and open to the moment. Thoughts, memories, and emotions are allowed to flow without judgment in and out of the mind. Some practices, like those taught by Ira Israel, adapt this open monitoring and add in labeling of negative and positive thoughts such as *that's my mind: fearing, remembering, regretting, reminiscing, desiring, planning, fantasizing, or wondering.* In this way, we can analyze where our thoughts are predominantly spending their time.

Mantras - A meditation that uses a repeated sound or word to focus the mind and prevent distraction. Original religious mantras had specific words with specific spiritual meanings, but more modern adaptations have used many types of words and sounds with great results.

Gratitude, Kindness, & Love - This meditation cultivates the heart-centered emotions of gratitude, kindness, and love. This is my favorite meditation for transitions because I've been doing it long enough that now when I close my eyes, I instantly feel immense and liberating gratitude and love.

Transcendental Meditation - Popularized by celebrities like The Beatles, this type of meditation involves exchanging money for a mantra based on your gender, birthday, and birth year. This idea that a guru holds the sole power to grant someone a proper mantra has not been well received, and in recent decades, practices with self-selected mantras have arisen.

Ancient Meditation Practices - There are many very specific types of Taoist, Yoga, and Zen meditation practices involving focuses on breathing, chakras (energy centers), emptiness, out of body, visualization, and more. One of the more recognized forms of these ancient meditation practices is trataka or gazing meditation where practitioners focus on a candle flame until their attention is complete, and then they close their eyes and mentally form the candle flame. This and the Taoist meditations on emptiness are similar to the concept behind the flame & the void mind exercise in Robert Jordan's international best-selling series *The Wheel of Time* — characters use the mental image of a flame and feed all their thoughts and emotion into it until they are empty and still inside the void.

Dr. Joe Dispenza's Meditation Adaptations - Author of *You Are The Placebo* and several other books on unlocking human potential through meditation, Dr. Joseph Dispenza first healed himself from a crippling accident and then went on a journey to understand how, going back to school for his PhD in the process, as well as conducting extensive research and testing on miraculous healings. He has a series of adapted meditations and each is amazing.

Dispenza's Changing Your Beliefs & Perceptions is my daily morning meditative practice. Only when I'm really out of sorts or short on time, do I start my day with the Release Meditation these days, but I'll use RM in the afternoon to squeeze in twenty minutes effectively. I don't think stopping 20 minutes into *Changing Your Beliefs & Perceptions* is beneficial; I've had to respond during that phase of the meditation a couple times, and my mind felt like unset clay, sagging without an artist's hand to guide it. I didn't like the way it felt at all, but in contrast, when I stay in the meditation through sensing the inside and outside of my body and then letting go of self, body, time, thought, and space, I have the opportunity to program myself with what I want to feel and what I want to fix about myself or my perception. These may be as simple as I want to stop worrying about money or I want to have Unstoppable Enthusiasm! Those are mine if you couldn't tell — but remember this is PRIVATE; you have complete control, so choose wisely and your highest self will respond. This meditation practice is guided, visualization-based, akin to self-hypnosis, and similar to zen meditations on emptiness. It is a potent blend of meditative best practices.

Dispenza's Blessing of the Energy Centers - Often misunderstood and called chakras in yoga traditions, energy centers, as Dr. Joe Dispenza calls them, are areas of our body that exude their own energy. Dr. Dispenza avoids the term chakras and labels and discusses these areas differently. Knowing our hearts are putting out a six to ten-foot electromagnetic field, it makes sense that other organs would have their own energy fields. This meditation focuses on each energy center in the body with gratitude and visualization, and it is incredibly invigorating. The following is based on the work of Dr. Joe Dispenza found in *Becoming Supernatural*.

Anyone who's been through puberty knows that their sexual organs have an energy field. What's interesting is our energy centers extend from around the base of our spine to above our head. That lust we feel in our sexual organs is directly next to and perhaps entangled with two other energy centers: your appetite for food and power. It is amazing when we realize that this pattern of overlapping appetites: sex, food, and power are all centered at the base of our spinal cord, which is an extension of our brain. We must be in control of these appetites, or they will drain our energy and derail progress on our goals. The next energy center above that is the space just below the sternum, it is where we carry our fears and anxieties. This is why courage lifts this part of our body literally, and why we crumple inward at this point when we are afraid.

The energy center above that is the heart, the most powerful part of our body electromagnetically. After letting go of fear and anxiety, this is where we open our hearts and feel love for all and for ourselves. When we have done this, the next energy center is our thyroid, which controls our metabolism, and it is the seat of our voice where we can speak the words we are holding in our hearts finally. The next energy center is in the middle of your brain — the pineal gland which releases melatonin and helps regulate our sleep. When we activate our pineal gland while in a meditative state, we can experience transcendent inspiration and even visions. The final energy center is 18 inches above the head and it is considered where divine inspiration distills upon us. *The Blessing of the Energy Centers* is a powerful guided meditation that involves visualization and progressive relaxation, so you finish your practice feeling whole and energized.

Dispenza's Kundalini Meditation is another yoga meditation technique. It is very interesting as it combines breathing, physical tension, and posture to draw up energy from the base of the spine, essentially from those base energy centers. This tension draws up the cerebrospinal fluid into the head. This is thought to rinse or flush the brain. The energy and even ecstasy that can flow from this technique are stunning.

I have not made these last two meditations daily practice, but I have done both many times. These ancient practices get results which can be verified via EEGs, blood panels, x-rays, cancer scans, etc. Dr. Dispenza has pushed innovation further with new technologies like the kaleidoscope vision movies and newer brain scanning and energy detection technologies, but never in substitute for current testing standards. His results are bold, proven, and continuing to improve.

Release Meditation - Brendon Burchard, author and high performance expert, has a simple 20-minute release meditation technique that is like transcendental meditation but without a secret word that costs money. Brendon's word is "Release," his technique is free, and it works extremely well. This is the first formal meditation I ever made into a daily practice, and it is still my touchstone when things are going wrong during my day. When I'm having trouble with other meditations, this is what I turn to.

It is important to know that your meditation experience will change as you wade further into your practice over time. When I began with Brendon Burchard's Release Meditation, it was like high-octane therapy. I've been through family therapy, marriage counseling, and multiple forms of 1:1 therapy with psychologists (talk therapy) and psychiatrists (drug therapy), but none of them had the efficacy of meditation. What happened changed my life, so I want you to be prepared for what might happen to you.

At first, meditation was amazingly easy. It was relaxing — I finally figured out a way to slow down and to enjoy being still for once in my life, but soon it became therapy, and then after many months of this, it became much harder to focus. Having multiple forms of meditation is how I stay focused, keep things fresh, and keep my daily practice going.

Guided Meditation - These are varied forms of recorded meditations with some as simple as listening along to affirmations or expressions of gratitude. Some are guided visualizations, self-hypnosis, and even brainwave training. Likely the most common guided meditations are those used to teach each type of meditation.

Visualization - When I was 6 years old, I began ski racing, and very soon into being coached, the concept of visualization came into play. The idea was simple: you'd envision yourself running the race, mastering a concept, or correcting a bad habit. Visualizing is simply seeing a picture of something in your mind and focusing on it. This simple meditation can get very complex depending on what you are visualizing.

Progressive Relaxation - When I first went off to boarding school in 7th grade, it was to a school for US ski team hopefuls, Killington Mountain School in Vermont. This can be a guided meditation, as it was for me initially, but you could do it by yourself easily too. By flexing and relaxing consciously each section of the body, we become very aware of our bodies, any injuries we might have, and also pathways or bridges to functionality.

Meditative Exercise - Qigong, yoga, tai chi, & more practices mix meditative states with physical movement. Other physical activities like distance running, dance, martial arts, and swimming can put us into a meditative zone of singular focus. Meditative exercise can also be the bridge from our resting meditative states to our daily lives. We all want the clarity and connection of our meditative states to carry into our daily lives, but many struggle with how to make that happen. Walking meditation and meditative exercises allow us to continue in that state with our eyes open.

Sensory Deprivation Meditation - Like a manual form of deep meditation, sensory deprivation chambers force us into a meditative state. For some folks, it can be extremely uncomfortable, but many have found it to be amazingly transformative and akin to powerfully transcendent meditation experiences.

Why Modern Adaptations?
Why are there so many modern adaptations of traditional meditation? Why can't we all honor the original forms and patterns? Many of us do not resonate with the religions attached to the older meditation forms. Are we missing the real experience? Dr. Joe Dispenza's research has proven that the beneficial processes of meditation are independent of their original religious context. He has been using modern brain, heart, and more monitoring systems to prove that these meditations are healing people of a whole spectrum of health problems including cancer and autoimmune diseases. They have seen their symptoms evaporate, their tumors shrink, and their lives change. These tests are also showing how these meditations work on the brain, breath, heart, and body's energy fields. While there's always something to be learned as we study original source material, it's clear that modern adaptations of ancient meditative practices aren't going anywhere and are proving their worth every day to more and more people all over the world.

Breathing

Breathing is something we often take for granted. It's always happening without us even trying, but it's our direct connection to each moment and our life. Becoming conscious of our breath alone has the ability to transform the moment. For some, meditation's most simple description is *attention to one's breath*. Truly feeling grateful for our breath alone can reduce us to tears. Breathing deeply oxygenates our blood and enlivens our body — it can even reduce and eliminate pain. Breathing is miraculous, and it took experiencing the worst pain in my life to figure it out on my own.

Remember that excruciating tooth pain I breathed and prayed away? The next day I saw the dentist, he did some work, and then I returned home to rest, but the day after that I woke up with a mind to look up two words: Wim Hof. I don't how I knew, but I knew I needed to look up Wim Hof, and

I knew it had something to do with what had happened the night before last. Watching him create a rhythm of very deep breathes akin to hyperventilation, then hold his breath as I did in the car that night was jaw-dropping — especially after hearing him describe how you NEVER should do the technique while driving! I immediately concluded that this was what my body was trying to do when I'd had all those panic attacks as a younger man. The numb hands, the pins and needles, and a deeper in-breath than out-breath were all familiar to me.

Pushing further through the pins and needles was NOT something I'd experienced before, and when I did, using the Wim Hof breathing method, I instantly understood why he felt like he could go in cold water: it felt like the pins and needles were pushed out to a topical layer on the skin itself, almost a shield. I took a cold shower and did not feel any pain. Do I take cold showers every day? I don't, but my wife ends every shower with cold water. There's an intensity to the Wim Hof breathing, cold shower, and physical stress regiment that I don't always resonate with, and that's okay. Not everyone likely can handle the Wim Hof breathing method at first, and that's why he has several warnings for folks starting out, so take it slow and mind your body and setting — you can find introductions to his work online and on youtube for free. For me most often, I like to be still and listen — it's this inverse to Wim Hof's breathing method that I enjoy as much or perhaps more.

Most recommendations when it comes to breathing, actually recommend something different from Wim Hof's method of rapid inhalation to maximum capacity followed by release, not fully out, and then repeating that 30—40 times, only to exhale and be without breath for one minute to several minutes, followed by inhaling and holding that breath for as long as possible. To change our heart rate and mindset, take a minimum of six long and deep breaths, hold each breath in for a count of ten or as close to ten as you can handle, and, each time, extend the exhale as you release that breath. This has a delicious quality to it where each breath grows longer than the last, stretching time and our experience in the moment.

Both breathing methods have their time and place, and there are many other breathing techniques out there.

I primarily learned to breathe diaphragmatically through the teachings of Roger Love, who as a teenager coached Earth, Wind, & Fire and the Beach Boys in the seventies, and later taught my good friend, bandmate, and producer, Peter Simon in Los Angeles, California. Peter, aka Jimmy Young aka Rasta, is an electrically charged enthusiast of the highest order, and he, using Roger Love's daily vocal warmup, taught me how to sing and breath over a decade ago. Up until that point, I'd been holding my breath, gasping, singing by sheer force, and extremely limited as a singer. Initially, I couldn't reach the ten minute marker in the twenty minute warmup, but I eventually did. It forced me to sing at a level I'd never been able to before, and it required me to breath deeply and quickly. When I finished the warmup, I was charged with confidence, oxygen, and enthusiasm. Peter and I would never go a performance without doing our vocal warmup together. I carried this over into my morning commute to my job as a high school teacher, and later, before I would go LIVE to over twenty thousand on Baker Creek Heirloom Seeds Facebook page, answering gardening questions in real-time, and today, before I film or record anything. Roger Love has online courses and his vocal warmups are found in various places online for free like Youtube.

4-4-8 Breathing is a common meditation breathing technique where one inhales to the count of 4, holds that breath for a count of 4, and then releases slowly to a count of 8. Some folks get breathless doing this and find that 3-3-6 works best for them. As with all breathing exercises, it changes as you improve — I find I prefer to do an 8-8-16 or even deeper set of breaths. At first, your Wim Hof experience will likely be very heady, and you may even blackout, but within days, it will become much more difficult to replicate the dizziness of the first day. I think this is why Wim Hof naturally became more active while using the breathing technique, so he could get even more oxygen into his system.

Our breathing can reveal what we are feeling, but can our breathing generate our emotions? Susana Bloch, author of *Alba Emoting: A Scientific Method for Emotional Induction*, mapped the breathing patterns of emotions and figured out that breathing is not just symptomatic of an emotion but can be used to create specific emotional states. Alba Emoting is breath training that focuses on generating desirable emotional states using breathing. Actors need only breath the pattern of fear, gratitude, elation, or anger to generate that emotion — forget the suffering and dangerous tendencies of method acting, we can breathe our way in and out of roles instead. For us all, this means our emotions are not only in our control but in the way we breathe.

Whatever you choose to try and experiment with, do so with care and attention: our breath is incredibly powerful, transformative, and healing.

Qigong *(Chi-gong)*

Qigong is an ancient Chinese practice that is a combination of meditation, exercise, and philosophy. It is rooted in the belief that our bodies contain a life energy called *chi* and that we can cultivate that energy through movement and thought. Tai Chi is similar but is widely recognized as a martial art. Though Qigong does contain some aspects of martial arts as well, it is seen as closer to exercise. I practice Qigong throughout my day during my transitions and within the first hour of waking. While it may look something akin to self-flagellation, it is enlivening the body when we strike ourselves in a very specific pattern. I strike myself with my fists, cupped hands, and palms while breathing deeply along my arms, shoulders, chest, back, hips, legs, and even torso. It is incredible for waking up fast, exponentially increasing awareness, and priming the body for action — it supercharges us. This is akin to martial artists slapping their thighs and chest before competitions or even a distant cousin of dry body brushing.

I have two Qigong exercises I do every day. One is intense; it starts first with knuckles, then closed hand (palm-side), and then slapping. This one covers nearly the entire body. I learned it from TJ Franks while watching E-Motion, the movie. The other exercise I do throughout my day, every hour, between transitions, or when I'm sore. Brendon Burchard showed me this one while I attended High Performance Academy LIVE in San Diego on that fated trip in late 2017, it's less intense but great for staying fresh and starting out. It's like the slapping stage of the first exercise, but instead, the hands are cupped and percussive. Legs are each cup clapped towards the heart, then the arms, sides, shoulders, and back. This alone was a game changer for me, so just because it's not as intense as the hitting Qigong, doesn't mean it isn't effective — I also have, at times, by accident given myself some pretty big bruises, so be careful! Less intense but using the same concept of physical touch to reset both body and mind, tapping is something I also use throughout my day.

Tapping

Linking many concepts together along with acupuncture and acupressure, tapping specific areas of the body is thought to unleash emotional and physical tension as well as to reprogram the mind and body with specific intentions. It is easy and anyone can do it.

My practice is very simple and learned again from Brendon Burchard at High Performance Academy LIVE: I tap with my fingers above my brows, on my cheekbones below my eyes, my upper lip, my chin, the back of my neck, the top of my head, behind my ears, and my chest. I tap each area 9 times while repeating 3 times aloud: Enthusiastic, Compassionate, Masterful. I form the emotions, concepts, and images associated with these words in my mind as I go through the exercise. There are other tapping practices out there that have more tapping locations and specific programs, but this simple technique is very powerful.

Something Tony Robbins said once has really stuck with me: we carry emotional signatures in our bodies that can be triggered when touched. This is why so often there is an emotional release from their patients when physical therapists do their work. The tension is both physical and emotional. His example was telling: imagine you're at your father's funeral and someone comes up beside you and slaps you on the shoulder and says, *I don't know how you are coping right now. I'd be a wreck if I was you.* Of course in that moment, that's crazy depressing, not what you need to hear, and now it's potentially encoded in your shoulder, so next time someone slaps you on the shoulder, even a year later, you go into a depressed, low energy state, and you don't even know why. This is also how hypnotists create triggers: my wife's grandfather hypnotized her aunt (his daughter), so that she could do a C-section operation without anesthesia. All she had to do was touch a certain spot on her leg, and she would lose all sensation from the chest down.

Yoga

Aspects of yoga have been mentioned in the meditation section, but I bring it up again to highlight the physical exercise practices which are many and range from ancient traditions to modern adaptations. I've been doing yoga for over a decade but did not become deeply committed to pushing my daily practice further until recent years. I initially learned from a yoga DVD from my wife's Grandpa Joe: *Yoga Zone* with Lisa Bennet and Charles Matkin. I've recently become acquainted with Lisa which is a bit surreal since her routine has been the core of my yoga practice every morning for twelve years. The routine itself was designed for beginners, so later on, when I encountered a in-person yoga teacher, Antoinette Marquez, I was, in her words, flexible but weak. I've been working on my strength ever since, and I've doubled my flexibility as a result.

Many of the more modern adaptations were created to accommodate weak students like myself, and while purists may insist that the religion should never have been parted from the exercises, the benefits of all forms of yoga are incredible and varied.

Dancing vs Jogging

Sometimes I start my day dancing. Even before I do yoga or Qigong, I'll be drawn to move. Now I'm not saying I'm a good dancer, but I love moving and feeling my body's full range. I love how my heart and breath reach a rhythm and intensity that changes my experience of the moment. I feel intensely, joyfully alive — I grin with abandon and delight. If I was to start a new hobby, it would likely be dancing. I need the cardiovascular conditioning, and I'm attracted to such a challenging whole body experience physically as well — I grew up doing judo and skiing. When I am excited, feeling good, and truly enthusiastic, I dance.

Sometimes before yoga and instead of dancing, I'll jog in place with my arms held high in the air above my head while lifting my knees as high as I can. This quickly gets tiring, and that's the idea. I want the hardest physical cardio workout priming to happen in the shortest amount of time, so when I kick into yoga I have my heart pumping my well-oxygenated blood into my muscles as I stretch. "Hardest" in this situation would be what's hardest for me without injury or strain. I don't get enthusiastic jogging in place like I do while dancing, but both prepare my body for yoga. I don't force myself to dance, so it only comes when I'm in my more enthusiastic states.

Outdoor Time

Growing up, being outside was the ultimate. I loved reveling in the smells, the life, and the weather. Growing up skiing also added to this. I was drawn to the woods as many are, but the health benefits from immersion in nature are so much greater than just enjoyment. They are long term and short term, subtle and dramatic.

Out in nature, we encounter the cleanest air, and that alone can be invigorating. Most cities do not produce their own oxygen; they don't have the trees to do so. Living as I do now in an area that is both coastal and has green plants year round, I've come to realize we are in a uniquely oxygenated environment — the plants here are photosynthesizing and releasing oxygen nearly year round, so the Pacific North West's temperate rainforest is releasing oxygen more often and at higher rates than other areas though when it does get snowy and icy, even evergreens go dormant. In contrast in winter, the Midwest's only oxygen is coming from the distant oceans.

While athletes may train in oxygen-deprived environments, to heal from very serious conditions we do the opposite: we raise oxygen levels in hyperbaric chambers. This was actually one of the treatment paths we were considering for my wife, and we regularly use activated oxygen topically. In composting, it is the oxygen, the aeration, that prevents the pile from becoming dangerous and unhealthy. Healthy soil is aerobic, filled with oxygen-loving microbes. We all love oxygen!

Contact with healthy soils have been proven to provide positive benefits, but this isn't surprising when we recognize that our gut and the soil are part of the same cycle and powered by very similar microbiology. Bacteria and fungi release and regulate the flow of nutrition to plant roots in the soil as they also do in our guts for our bodies: humans cannot digest their food without help from bacteria and fungi. By just touching the soil, some soil bacteria can even trigger the release of serotonin!

The majesty and scope of nature itself are humbling and inspiring. When we immerse ourselves in nature, we see our small corner of the universe and our rightful place in a much larger and more profound orchestra of life than we were taught about in high school and college. Working with nature is humbling and inspirational as well — it's also incredibly powerful. It can heal us from the brink of despair working with animals, plants, fungi, and even soil life. They all are ALIVE and respond to your interaction. There's a precious sweetness to generating more life on this earth while we are here. Sometimes folks who have never gardened wonder why people talk to their plants or see them as their children. When you've been caring for and then been taken care of by nature; the reciprocity pricks the heart. You realize some fundamental truths. I'm breathing those plants breath. My body is the soil. My health relies upon collaborative communities of microbiology in the soil and inside me. I am everything and everything is me.

When I was upset as a teen, I'd often go for walks or runs in the woods alone. The peace of the woods would always open my heart to wonder, awe, and enthusiasm again. Nature always brings me back to myself. Today as I work, I pause and gaze out the window at the trees and the sunlight playing through the snow covered branches, and it stirs my heart.

There is a Lakota tradition of greeting the dawn to show honor and give thanks for the new day directly to the rising sun. You might thank the universe, God, or Heavenly Father for the sun, but expressing it first thing in the morning is like recognizing our breath. This one simple thing that comes and goes, with or without us paying any attention, is the sole reason we get to enjoy another day. Be grateful for this world, for this body, for the earth, for the sun, and for all life, and you will find enthusiasm and love for all course through you unstoppably.

Silence & Listening

The stillness we cultivate in meditation is often only found when we are meditating in a quiet space. Silence is grounding in its own way — it connects us to the moment in solemn intimacy such that we claim the silence for our own when we find it. We'd be pained if someone broke it because in the silence can we truly listen to that which is sacred, the still small voice of our enthusiasm. When you find yourself in a silent place, do you listen? What do you hear? I often hear: *I love you.* When I write in this book, I listen as I write. My fingers follow along as the voice in my head speaks. So often, authors speak of finding their voice, and it's true, we have to find that authentic voice that emanates from our deepest selves, to listen, and to write it down on paper — only to read it back to ourselves and see if it resonates still with that inner space.

I wake up between 5 am & 6 am every day, so I can enjoy the silence, listen, and grow closer to who I am inside. My wife prefers the end of the night to be hers and hers alone without any distraction. While some advocate the usage of headphones, their damaging effects on hearing are well documented, and everyone prefers to not wear them given the option.

You've likely heard of silent meditation retreats where participants will go weeks even months without speaking. While it is not for everyone, this extreme silence and listening activity can also have powerful benefits: many artists and authors use these types of retreats as inspiration for their next project. Many find it brings immense peace, deeper insight, and greater self-love, but we don't need to go to a retreat to have silence tomorrow, we can instead go to bed a bit earlier and wake up a bit earlier, or go on a walk and find a quiet place to sit. We all can find time and place for silence and listening.

Priming with External Triggers

Watching a motivational video on Youtube primes me like little else does. I get PUMPED! I get focused, motivated, and enthusiastically charged with energy. If I listen to certain songs, they have very specific effects on me, and I've built them into triggers by listening to them daily for months and, in some cases, years on end. I have visual cues all over the house as well. I have my goals posted on the wall next to me over my calendar. I have Trailblazer, Lynchpin, Exemplar on a light-up sign on my desk — I tap in those three words just before lunch every day. I have inspiring questions and statements all over my house that help me stay focused — you, too, might place things strategically that inspire you around your home, office, or workspace.

Priming with Visualization

Tony Robbins talked about visualizing to prime his mind for a few minutes every morning, and I realized this is exactly what almost every athlete is doing before their turn or moment. This is how they get into the zone. I have a series of visions I visualize. They are related to my goals, short and long term, as well as my enthusiasm. When times are hard, I visualize these moments as well as moments from my past like performing for thousands, getting married, or holding my newborn sons. Before I go out to speak, I often visualize going out onto bigger stages to raise my necessity and change my state to match where I want to go not where I am currently — it also makes any size audience seem smaller and more intimate. I want my message to transcend that medium and create a moment. As mentioned earlier, if we can visualize it to the point of emotionally connecting to the experience, it tricks our brain into believing it is experiencing the visualization in real-time. Visualizing prepares us for that a reality, and many argue that through visualization, we make that reality more likely, but is that true?

Future Writing

When we write out a prophecy or a prediction for the future, it may or may not come true. This is true, but it's also equally true that everything around us in our world was first an idea in someone's head, and most of those ideas were fleshed out on paper first. Predictions, prophecies, science fiction, goals, dreams, and future writing of all sorts have a strong tendency to come true over a long enough course of time because strongly held ideas and beliefs are contagious, and if enough minds hold the same idea of something to come, an expectation builds and it, in some form, becomes a reality. If we do nothing and plan nothing, we can be certain nothing will occur, but if we take action, believing anything is possible, and cast our will into future with the best of intentions, we have the best opportunity to make it happen.

Many successful people today cite the Law of Attraction as the cornerstone of their success. It's a practice that is based on visualizing and emotionally connecting to your dream future to attract that future wealth, love, or success. There are also many critics of the Law of Attraction and the book, *The Secret*, because there is more to the story.

The Law of Attraction's Caveat

If you are a fan of *The Secret* or the Law of Attraction, you likely have recognized elements of those concepts in my work, but I didn't study those things until rather recently. What I've always known is that preparation is the only way opportunity doesn't turn into regret. If you are anything like me, you've had opportunities you've not prepared for and watched them sail off into the sunset without you. While it is true that focusing on what we want in life draws it to us, it is also true that if we do not put in the work, we will not be able to appreciate those blessings.

> Faith without works is Dead
> ~James 2.26

We can't just hope and wish for things to get better. We have to put the work in. Every morning we have a choice to make: What kind of day will it be? Use the **Morning Ritual Menu** to craft your own personalized series of rituals. Expand and explore when you have the time, or focus on a few when times are tight, but begin your journey tomorrow morning!!

How long is all this going to take?

Ideally, the first hour of our day should always be sacred and set apart for resetting and priming ourselves for the day. Sometimes I take over an hour, but then I begin to shrink my daily planning and best creative writing time periods. I use Brendon Burchard's research-based High Performance Planner for planning my day, blocking out my times of work, and staying aligned with my goals and high performance habits. I always have a notebook for gratitudes, notes, and miscellaneous in addition to my planner wherever I go. I start and finish my working day with my planner and my notebook. Planning can take 15-20 minutes or 3 hours depending on where I am in terms of planning and execution of one of my plans. Somedays I spend an entire day planning, priming, and visualizing to create the kind of future I want, but usually, that is once a month. I try to let the process lead, to listen to the song that is being sung, rather than try to mark the time or get on with things.

The Morning Ritual Menu
Pick Your Golden Hour Offering!

Gratitudes

Meditation & Prayer

Affirmations

Breathing

Qigong

Tapping

Yoga

Dancing (or Jogging)

Outdoor Time

Silence & Listening

Priming with External Triggers

Priming with Visualizations

Future Writing

Daily Planning

Download & Print It Out:
www.matt-powers.mykajabi.com/p/unstoppablereaders

The Daily Rituals

The Hourly Break

The first time I heard classical union musicians were guaranteed hourly breaks I thought it was crazy, but later as I grew older and wiser, I understood how vital taking breaks is to sustaining high performance. I was gigging regularly at the time and always wanted to play longer, just a few songs more on that stage. Nights, I'd want them to last forever in my youth — I'd stay up for days trying to chase those fleeting feelings of wonder and awe. I was young and experiencing so much of life for the first time in NYC. Later after college, I would work three to six jobs at a time, all part-time, but some shifts would connect, and I'd be pulling two to three days a week working all day and all night between nightclubs, catering gigs, and Philip Van Heusen/Calvin Klein's midtown offices. I'd regularly collapse in closets for twenty-minute naps in piles of Calvin Klein shirts or on piles of unclaimed coats in the back of a coat check. The energy it required to live this way was immense. My light would regularly dim from the abuse, and I'd sleep deeply for 18+ hours.

I became more acquainted with healthier concepts of work once I became a teacher and saw for myself how people learn best and, later even more so, through Brendon Burchard's *High Performance Habits*. Now I have alarms that go off on my phone every hour with a trigger song and an activity or series of activities that I have to do. I regularly change the song out to keep it fresh, because, after a month or so, you might just find yourself ignoring the alarms as I do… OR you might do the opposite and anticipate them, getting up out of your chair and starting a Qigong exercise only to have the alarm go off as you are doing it. It will be different for everyone and may even be different for you at different times of your life, but start taking a break.

What do we do during our hourly break?
We can reprise shortened versions of our morning routine, to reset and prime, so we can start another hour ready for anything. This is like training our muscles for any task or like training a horse; it is the consistent repetition that wins the day. It takes persistence, but it's possible to carry and return to our morning mental spaces literally: we can return to our meditative brain wave states in just moments after only months of training, and over years of repetition, those meditative brain states begin to show up without meditation or the eyes being closed. Thus we can train our minds like a muscle for enthusiasm and then prime and reset throughout our day, training that muscle to be reflexive and available to us all day long. Not only are we setting a course for a new life, but we are guiding it and doing the work every step of the way. This victory is ours completely, and it is a gift of joyful enthusiasm we get to share with everyone.

You may take a moment to pray, to give thanks, or to be silent and still once an hour. You may get up and jog or do jumping jacks. It may be Qigong with your eyes closed and a full glass of water like me. I try to remember to close my eyes regularly, but I also tend to get into a gazing meditative zone where I type as fast as I think or speak. When I'm in this zone, it's like I'm watching my thoughts form on the screen, but after a few hours of screen time, it takes a toll on the eyes. Resting my eyes has been such an easy solution to strain, headaches, and tension. Breaks are so powerful, they give us the recharge to go longer and smarter, so over time we become stronger and go farther than we ever could have under a boom and bust model of working.

But what if you are in the middle of something?
While some will say, you ALWAYS obey the alarm; others have children, loved ones that need help when they need it, a role in a system that needs their complete focus at times, or are LIVE on camera at times, but we can adjust, snooze, shift, and adapt. The idea is simple: take a break every 50–

60 minutes and you will improve your performance, connection, and creativity over time exponentially.

The Transition

How we handle transitions directly correlates to how sustainable our energy is throughout the day. When we sit, we often flex to have good posture or we slouch and put tension on different areas — both habits need release regularly. This hourly break can be your chance to avoid that back pain, that stiff leg, or that knot in your neck. You may find your hands and wrists don't ache as much too. Use this time to release the tension, to reset your mind, and to prime yourself both physically and mentally for the next hour, task, and role.

Smiling

Over and over, studies show the benefits and power of smiling to transform our mindsets and mood. This occurs even if we start with a forced smile — our bodies just can't help but follow along. Smiling releases serotonin, dopamine, and endorphins. It's also naturally infectious. While some folks may feign they are immune, everyone is drawn to a smile.

Gratitude

This can be as simple as saying thank you with our eyes closed in a meditative state for 30-60 seconds every hour. You may look at family photos, message a sincere thank you to someone who's had an impact on your life, read a passage from an inspirational book, watch a video on gratitude, or listen to an audio recording or audiobook. We can spark our gratitude purposefully, again and again, learn our nooks and crannies, and seek out our emotional deep ends. We can become sensitized to gratitude throughout our day until it is habit and part of the way we transition between activities, how we handle interruptions, and how we manage challenges.

Meditation & Visualization
This can be a shortened version of the Release Meditation, as I do, or it could be any of the meditations listed that you are comfortable with. After letting go, visualize the next hour or activity. See yourself successfully accomplishing it. Feel the satisfaction and gratitude — the joy of seeing it done.

Qigong
Qigong has the dual effect of releasing tension and focusing the mind. Using it hourly, I find it keeps me loose and helps me get back on track, especially energetically. Later in the day, it's the Qigong breaks that get me through.

Psychological Cues

These transitions, if handled poorly, can jeopardize our relationships, our marriages, our businesses, and our health. If we manage these transitions well, we can transform them into opportunities to cultivate enthusiasm. It is one of the best ways to nurture our relationships, marriages, businesses, and healthy habits.

The Car trigger
Every time we get into a car, we have an opportunity to pause and make a powerful habit. You might put inspirational words on your dashboard or on your keychain to remind you, but every time you get into that car you can feel gratitude for being alive. Maybe it's when you are about to leave the car or, more specifically, before you leave the car after coming home from work.

The Wallet Trigger
Maybe your wallet or purse has a special significance you've attached to it, maybe you have words on it, or maybe you have a picture on it to remind

you of that significance. If we can transform your wallet to carry an enthusiasm trigger, every time you make a purchase or take out your ID, you are reminded of why you are unstoppably enthusiastic. If you are thinking, *I don't like to think about money; it stresses me out*, then please turn that negative trigger into a positive one and start feeling gratitude every time you see that purse or wallet. It will not only change your relationship to money, but it might just help you get out of the way of earning a whole lot more as was my experience.

The Bathroom Mirror Trigger

The bathroom mirror is an intimate space. Some of us hardly look at ourselves. Some of us can't stop looking at ourselves… sadly, most of the people in this category are not looking at themselves with kindness. There is a campaign by Marisa Peers for people, especially women, to write *I Am Enough* in lipstick on their mirrors. In her work, she has over and over found that thinking we are not enough is the root of many psychological and even physical problems. She recommends continuously repeating *I Am Enough* to ourselves aloud and in our heads throughout our day because over time our conscious mind and subconscious, the body, accept the statement as true, and, often times, challenges that were once crippling instead, in overcoming them, help them rise to a new level in their performance or self. I absolutely love this concept and have an adapted mirror trigger where anytime I'm in front of the bathroom mirror I say: *I Love You, I'm Proud of You, You Are Enough*. It's a practice that makes me smile and brings me back to my enthusiasm.

The Door Trigger

When we walk through any doorway, we have an opportunity to remind ourselves of who we are. You may recall the words you tap in during your morning routine *Enthusiasm, Compassionate, Masterful*, a priming powerful phrase like *I Am Enough!* or *You Got This!*, or you may simply train yourself to feel a burst of confidence every time you pass through a doorway. This last one I'm working on. Though we live in a smaller home currently, there are 14 doorways in it (even the bathroom has two doors). By taking something that is common and repetitive in my life and turning it into a trigger, my everyday life can become an experience of exponential growth and deeper meaning. Every doorway we walk through we get to decide how we enter that room: with a smile or with stress.

Timers & Clocks
Your cell phone, computer, alarm clock, and more can provide regular reminders to pause from work, reset yourself, and prime your enthusiasm. I use my cell phone and regularly rotate the music. My friend, Kai Sawyer, has a mindfulness clock that chimes hourly. Every time it sounds he pauses his life, closes his eyes, and focuses on his breath.

Reconnect All Day Long

Echoing pieces of your morning ritual will allow you to shake off the fog and return to yourself, your best self, again in moments with practice. It takes making these breaks a habit that you embrace fully. You can do it. It may be hard at first. It may be a relief. It may feel unnatural to stop the flow. It may feel awkward to withdraw or interrupt, but know that it is the path you are building with each break, priming, and resetting that will build the bridge to your unstoppable enthusiasm. It is what will transform your path, your life, your business, and your relationships, so it is worth it to do the work and make it a habit.

The Daily Ritual Menu
Take ACTION! BE UNSTOPPABLE!!

Smiling

Gratitudes

Meditation & Prayer

Affirmations

Breathing

Qigong

Tapping

Dancing

Visualization

Psychological Cues

REMEMBER WHO YOU ARE

Download & Print It Out:
www.matt-powers.mykajabi.com/p/unstoppablereaders

The Evening Ritual

How are you closing your evening? Many of us are putting ourselves to sleep with the tv, social media, or Netflix, but is that healthy? Does that help or hinder our sleep? You likely have already heard about blue lights suppressing our melatonin secretion, but this is more than that. What are we filling our minds within those last hours of the day? Did you know that our brain waves are in a similar state as they are in the early morning? We are so close to sleep that we can easily shift into an alpha brain wave state. It is a time that many meditate, pray, reflect on their day, write in their journals, read, and prepare themselves for the next day. Some do yoga, others practice Qigong, others take a walk as a family, and some spend time reflecting on their day as a group. Evening resetting and priming practices help us let go of the frustrations and failures from our day and help us focus on the future with faith, the past with gratitude, and the present with peace.

The evening is a time for preparing the mind & body for the restoration that comes with sleep. Properly preparing for sleep is critical to maximizing its potential. Being gentle and reverent with our evenings can turn the close to each day into something sacred and meaningful. Avoid eating before bed. Avoid screens and over stimulation. We are slowing our bodies and minds down, so in many ways, we are doing the opposite of what we were first thing in the morning. All the exercises are to soothe, settle, and relax. It is a time that allows for gentle resetting and priming before we release our conscious hold of our day and dip into the deepest levels of our minds.

Yoga
Evening yoga is very different from morning or day-time yoga's conditioning, strengthening, and energizing effects on our bodies. Instead, the role of practicing yoga before we go to bed is to release tension, calm the mind, improve circulation, slow the breath, reclaim the body's energy,

and slow the heart rate. There are many evening yoga practices, but often the same poses are used — just the approach and manner in which we do them is different. Listen to your body. You may already have a yoga routine for the night, or you may just adopt a light stretching routine that improves your circulation and allows your body to reset and relax deeper but find what helps you get healing rest.

Qigong

Like yoga, the invigorating Qigong practices have their evening options as well. These, too, are designed to prepare the mind and body for rest. Because Qigong is focused on our chi, the life force energy of our body and the universe, it is an act of gathering energy in, collecting ourselves before we rest. There are simple and more complex practices. Some simply focus on breathing while others involve a slow, gathering motion before laying down to sleep. There is also a Qigong type of body scan meditation where we travel through our body with our minds and pay attention to each area. Just resting our attention on an area will allow it to relax and for more blood and oxygen to reach that area. Because I tend to never lay down in bed unless it is time to go to sleep, I fall asleep usually within minutes of laying down, so I rarely feel drawn to do a body scan or meditation.

An Evening Stroll

Something that can happen earlier in the evening is going on a walk alone or with loved ones to end the day, to connect, to create a clear break from work, and to relax. Touching base with nature, breathing fresh air, moving our bodies in a gentle liberating way, and getting closer with the people who mean the most to us clears our minds of stress and helps us focus on what matters. This is one of my favorite activities, but it's also one of the ones that gets skipped all too often.

Review & Assessments
I have my notebook and my orange High Performance Planner out. My computer is off, the pen is snug between my middle and index finger as I write, the lights are dimmed, and I'm looking over my day and my schedule for tomorrow through the lenses of my calendar and the planner. What did I get done? What were today's wins? How am I doing in regards to my weekly & monthly goals? How did I do on the Daily Habits Scorecard in the Planner? Am I ready for tomorrow? This can be less relaxing and more stressful if we've not had the kind of day we planned or desired, but this is exactly the time you decide to make it different tomorrow. You commit, and put it to rest: it's done. Doesn't matter that it hasn't happened yet, it's a guarantee now, so you can let it go, and move on to the next stage. While it may seem like we are letting the tiger out of the cage for a bit, we need to acknowledge our failures, stresses, and fears if we are to address them with solutions rooted in unstoppable enthusiasm — those concerns left untended grow and manifest in other ways, so put them to bed before you go to bed.

Gratitude Journaling
Do you have a journal? What kind of journal?
Is it a record of your day or is it the refinement of your day?
When we look back on our day and search for reasons to be grateful, we deemphasize the stress and amplify our gratitude.

> For years I've advocated keeping a gratitude journal, writing down five things every day that brought pleasure and gratefulness.
> ~Oprah Winfrey

Writing down our daily gratitudes also influences how we store our memories from the day. Glial cells are responsible for a whole host of critical activities in our brains, including clearing out toxins and encoding memory at the end of each day — they are impaired by irregular or a lack of sleep. This mean stress can affect our memory if it affects our sleep. We can work with our glial cells and give them the seven to nine hours of sleep they need to do their important work, but we can also influence them further with the way in which we reflect. We can select the best memories from our day to highlight, and we can reframe them for maximum gratitude and growth — this sets the tone for our sleep and for our next day.

While we don't do it every night, we certainly try to, as a family, write down three things we are grateful for after dinner. We each take a turn sharing while my wife records in our family gratitude journal. The process of sharing is relaxing and brings us closer together as a family as we express our gratitude for the day.

Over time, challenges, conflicts, and even failures and great loss are seen as part of a larger picture. We see a long chain of lessons, growth, and gratitude that make up our lives. We begin to cherish our days and see them for what they are: each one a gift. This is truly the path to unstoppable gratitude as well: developing a reflexive habit of recognizing life's blessings in our day. Just like how the meditative brain waves states can extend past the meditation after years of practice, so too can gratitude become a state of being that infuses the entire day, our whole heart, and the fullness of our minds.

We each are vessels — what are you filling yourself with?

What Time's Bedtime?

Is there a universal bedtime for all human beings? Arnold Schwarzenegger has encouraged those seeking success to sleep less than seven to nine hours: *Sleep faster* and get more hours out of every day, but does it really work that way? Can we be effective with only four to six hours of sleep a night consistently? Or is that a fragile tactic? Is that stoppable? Does that kindle enthusiasm and resilience? Isn't that the way exhaustion creeps in and then gives us a "cold"? For me, I only get sick when I'm pushing myself past my limits physically and mentally. I've begun to see these sick times as consequences for cheating myself of regular rest. I try to go to bed at or around 10 pm every night, and I try to avoid screens for at least an hour before bed, but if I don't slow down early enough, I end up like a train that didn't apply the brakes early enough, the inertia carries me right past that 10 pm station. This momentum is self-defeating on a long enough time-scale. If I go to bed at 11 pm too many nights in a row, I end up with a low-level baseline of irritation which can manifest as distraction, confusion, misinterpretation, and even assumption. Needless to say, when this happens or begins to happen, I do my best to get back on track that night.

When I'm able to get to sleep before 10 pm for three nights in a row, an undeniable spark and readiness bubble up from inside me, and I feel

AMAZING!! I wake up ecstatic for the new day. I wake before the alarm does. I joyfully grin my way through the morning affirmations, feeling the words deeply. Song lyrics jump out at me. I am more sensitive to people's emotions. I can see what needs my wife and children have. Getting enough rest, seven to nine hours a night, changes how our bodies feel and our minds perceive the world.

If you cringe at the thought of sleeping that much, consider this: if you really want to dive deep, go further than this and try splitting your sleep into two four-hour chunks, waking in the middle of the night for an hour. Think this is too wild? History has shown us that before the electric light, this is how we slept. We'd fall asleep 1–2 hours after sunset, wake in the middle of the night, write, pray, make love, discuss our dreams, visit neighbors, and then we'd return to bed for another short sleep. The literary and historical records are filled with references to the midnight hour — they were not referring to 12 am, but the hour we would wake between first and second sleep. I used to have my high school students read a BBC article called *The Myth of the Eight-Hour Sleep* about sleep experiments conducted with participants experiencing the Arctic's disorienting sunless time periods. They all settled into a bimodal sleep pattern. There are even historical accounts of doctors telling mothers to break their children of bimodal sleep patterns, and it wasn't motivated by health concerns but social and economic ones instead: they wanted more working hours out of workers. The bimodal sleep pattern was seen as inefficient, and within a generation, it was programmed out of us. It's time to take a second glance at the way we sleep and decide how we'd like to live.

I've tried to listen to the advice of Russel M. Nelson, current president of the Church of Jesus Christ of Latter-Day Saints, and when I wake up at 3 am or 4 am with mental clarity and a singing heart, I get out of bed, go into a separate room, take out a pen and paper, and then I get quiet and listen. I always have insights — sometimes they are just for me, and sometimes I share them with my family. Sometimes they even play into my work — some of this book has been written in that midnight hour.

Listening to our bodies might lead us to sleep even more. During this time period of healing, Adriana, my wife, is sleeping twelve to fourteen hours a day. She feels like life is hurtling by her, but she is healing. I want to add that quality over quantity matters because when we are truly in the moment, time slows, and minutes, hours, and seconds don't have the same meaning. Slow time, honor time, and give yourself the time to make your enthusiasm unstoppable.

Imagine Yourself...

You are now living the rituals. You wake eager to start your morning ritual. You may start the moment your feet touch the floor, or you might sneak away to another room to be private. You know what to expect, and so does your body: you are filled with enthusiasm as you fall into a routine of deep meaning and fulfillment before your day even begins. You then coax that fire within you throughout the day, keeping it bright, and keeping the doubts at bay or, at least, keeping them moving on. You then finish your day enveloped in gratitude and joy for your life and the day you just experienced. You embrace rest with the eager excitement of a child before Christmas and peace of one who's worked a full day to satisfaction. This is you. This is your life now, and you can go anywhere with your enthusiasm shining brightly.

The Evening Ritual Menu
Pick Your Reflection Hour Offering

Gratitude Journal

Meditation & Prayer

Evening Yoga

Evening Walk

Breathing to Slow & Relax

Qigong

Planning & Prophecy

Reading

Review & Assessments

Download & Print It Out:
www.matt-powers.mykajabi.com/p/unstoppablereaders

Enthusiastic Action

Now that you are in the daily rhythm of living the resetting and priming habits of unstoppable enthusiasm, we can take specific enthusiastic action to ramp things up. We may not be able to do these daily or even weekly, but they are powerful catalysts for going deeper, keeping our fire hot, and expanding our repertoire. You might take up dancing, start a gym membership, or organize a local group centered around one of your enthusiasms. The dream is yours to dream.

Deliberate Practice

Practice makes perfect... or does it not? While we've all heard practice praised consistently: ten thousand hours of practice, and we'll be a master, but is that true? In fact, it has been disproven. That ten thousand-hour marker was an average, not the spectrum. What has been proven, since the ten thousand-hour rule became widely adopted, is that we can master skills in shockingly short periods of time. How can this be? What could we have been doing wrong? The difference is in deliberate practice, a concept beautifully articulated in the book *Peak* by Robert Pool and Anders Ericsson. Measuring ourselves consistently and working on consistent improvement, especially small consistent daily improvements, defines deliberate practice, but it may look very different in different contexts. Athletes may be reviewing the video of that day's practice with their coach in preparation for tomorrow's focus. Some weightlifters, always think in terms of *Just One More*. It could be a rep, a set, a lap, a pushup, or pound, but it's something taken one step further that day. Like many of these concepts and sections, they touch upon other areas of the book: deliberate practice is as much about the mindset as it is about the action.

There is a concept in psychology called the Confidence/Competence Loop which is directly linked to deliberate practice. When we gain competence in anything, we gain confidence in our knowledge and skills in that area. Deliberate practice's consistent improvement model trains the mind for confidence with its small wins and daily persistence. If we want more confidence, we need to be more deliberate about our practice.

My own experience has been that all high performers utilize deliberate practice, and I've never seen anything different. When I was young, my dad would record us ski racing, and we'd review the tapes with him. Later, we'd review tapes with our coaches at Killington Mountain School. Musicians are relentless in their pursuit of deliberate practice — the best play like they are always on stage:100% ON. They record themselves, narrow down on their weakness, improve that area, and then do it again.

To improve always takes reflection, an examination of what we can change to do better. If we cannot film or record ourselves, let's write the words out and read them — aloud is best! After each statement, asking ourselves *Is this true?* can open ourselves up to even greater insight. We also can present or discuss our ideas with friends, mentors, or family to get the feedback we need, but be careful with who you ask for feedback: sometimes the wrong kind of feedback can hurt more than help. Choose folks you trust who will help you improve even in the midst of your greatest blunders. If we can hold onto our growth mindsets, we can use deliberate practice and reflection to push things further and forward.

Asking Questions

The highest level of learning is teaching, but Heuristic teaching is the highest level of teaching. Socratic methods of teaching involve a teacher asking questions that stimulate student participation and the asking of more questions. Heuristic methods go further: students ask the stimulating questions, and the teacher facilitates their journey towards understanding and, ultimately, wisdom. It is a fundamental shift for the student role from passive to active. We can finally feel the reality: that we are responsible and accountable for our own development. This becomes fuel for our enthusiasm — while it may read like something onerous, it is delightsome to the heart and mind to pursue our curiosity and construct our own understanding of the world through exploration.

Mentioned earlier, but also echoed in Dean Graziosi's book *Millionaire Success Habits*, asking why repeatedly, going 7 *Why's Deep*, allows us to shift from our conscious mind's quick automated reply to our heart's more authentic and honest answers. I recently filmed myself on camera doing this exercise for a re-shoot of *Regenerative Entrepreneurs & Experts*, one of my online courses — it's critical to know your deepest why when trying to start a business, a nonprofit, or teach. You have to be strongly rooted because those paths are stormy and not without great challenge, but therein lies the reward: we get to feel that congruency from our deepest why to our daily actions and intent. Integrity, self-respect, and self-confidence are key ingredients to unstoppable enthusiasm.

How can I bring enthusiasm to this moment? For ourselves, for each other, and for all life, how can we change the world around us to be sweeter? What can we do? Asking questions is often the action to take first, but even after we get going, they help keep us on task, in alignment with our goals, and enriching our relationships with others, ourselves, our enthusiasm, and the natural world.

Walking & Talking

Do you have an enthusiastic way of talking? What about walking? Remember walking meditations? The concept is all the same: maintaining meditative states outside the context of sitting, standing, and laying down. If we are training our minds for enthusiasm, we need to also train our bodies. First, imagine what walking enthusiastically feels like and then visualize yourself walking with unstoppable enthusiasm. Step into that vision and begin to walk around the room. As you make this a habit, you can practice it at any time by just bringing your attention to your walk. The same is true of talking. Can you envision yourself talking enthusiastically? Not in an overbearing way, but in a way that shares and spreads enthusiasm within the conversation. Asking sincere questions, sharing your own enthusiasms, showing compassion, and finding commonalities can amplify enthusiasm in any conversation.

You might go for a walk every morning or evening and practice walking enthusiastically. You might shoot videos practicing speaking and walking enthusiastically, and watch yourself afterward, honor your wins, and learn from your mistakes. We can walk the walk and talk the talk — it just takes time, persistence, and deliberate practice.

Dressing the Part

Do you have a favorite outfit? That one shirt that makes you feel like *Now I'm ready to go out!* It might be a hat, a dress, a jacket, a pair of shoes, or a pair of overalls if you're anything like me. When I put on a pair of overalls, I'm stepping into my role as a permaculture and gardening teacher — it's my superhero cape and mask; it's that transformative. I also have sweatsuit onesies — I can attest that they do not inspire superhero-like action while being worn. You might have an outfit that catapults you into a certain role or mental space too, or you could craft one. I've seen this many times as a musician: musicians settle on a look and then wear that look until it becomes their persona and their costume.

What can we galvanize with meaning?

Play

One of the most fundamental and powerful ways to amplify our enthusiasm is to play. This is something quite rare these days — even among children.

> Play, by definition, is self-controlled and self-directed.
> ~Peter Gray

Not only is it an expression of individuality and choice, but play is also the cornerstone of our adaptability as a species. Play is how children learn to become adults — it's how we learn the skills we need socially, physically, and environmentally. Humans deprived of play suffer in many ways including a decreased ability to solve problems that are new to them. There is also a link to violence and the prevention of childhood play, so play is hardly trivial. Instead, play is the ultimate schema builder — it is how we bundle smaller skills into larger skills and abilities. When we play with something, we explore all possibilities, pour our enthusiasm into it, and take pleasure in that exploration.

We jump, skip, sprint, laugh, climb, fiddle, and act silly. We smile our deepest, breath our hardest, and express ourselves with the most creativity when at play. It is magical because we are fully in the moment, living in joy, and pushing ourselves to our limits. Most of us have not grown up with enough time playing, and that can be holding us back. Play can increase creativity, release tension, and build resilience and skill. Take time for unstructured, non-goal oriented play.

Exercise & Sports

After years of avoiding exercise, I've found that it is key to my enthusiasm, and the lack of it was the source of my physical pain in my back, neck, and shoulders for over a decade. I started skiing when I was only two years old, and I do not remember a time when skiing wasn't natural to who I was and how I thought. By the time I was in high school, I was training year-round alongside US ski team prospects and future Olympians, and this was no accident. My father's dad was supposed to be in the 1940 Olympics, but that was the year it was canceled due to WWII. My dad saw Olympic potential in all his boys, or at least, that's the impression I got as I struggled to keep up with my two older, star-athlete brothers. What I never understood during this time period was that I was laying down a strong foundation for my life's health and even my enthusiasm. I was just trying to please my parents and brothers enough to get approval. I wasn't even playing to win — I was playing to get approval, and because of that I never tasted the full benefits of all the work I did. I didn't look within, so it didn't feed that part of me.

This is critically important: don't make workouts torture, make them rapturous and joyous instead. HOW? Find what liberates you physically through exercise or sports and follow that path.

Today I have a daily practice of yoga and Qigong, and a sometime practice of walking, hiking, kayaking, and running. I need the latter, cardiovascular workouts, to become a bigger part of my repertoire for certain, but only through the work of yoga and Qigong in conjunction with a very unique and brilliant chiropractor and sensory system expert, Dr. David Merrill, have I found myself ready to take on that physical activity. Years of no exercise and endless hours of playing bass live and in the studio had warped my shoulders and back, but now things are dramatically different — my back and posture have never been better. I'm still working on my shoulder, but I've never been as holistically strong or healthy in my entire life.

Why does it work? Hormetic stress = growth = self respect. When you put in the time and effort to earn your own respect, there's a deep congruency that people can sense from a mile away. Hormetic stress is the sweet spot for challenging yourself: it's not abusive and not too easy. You learn every time, and it forces you to progress. This is exactly what star athletes do. For ourselves, the stress leads to self-respect, more resiliency, real growth, and, if done in a rapturous way, true ebullient joy. We can punish ourselves with exercise, or we can deeply nourish ourselves with it — the choice is ours, and it has the potential to launch our lives into new levels of experience.

Does this mean we should go out and go wild? Not at all — listen to your body, follow your joy, challenge yourself but don't hurt yourself, and, if need be, consult your doctor, chiropractor, or physical therapist before you take on a new physical activity. You might start with daily walks for twenty to thirty minutes, and that would be an improvement, or you could be like me and have a secret desire to learn to dance, not to perform or compete but to feel my body's full strength and potential in full expression of physical joy.

Singing, Music, & Dance

Music has the ability to cut through our mental blocks and debris and reconnect us with a memory, a feeling, or an idea. In recent years, music has been used with seniors in nursing homes who hadn't spoken for years. The results have been dramatic — individuals light up, they smile, wide-eyed, and they talk, sometimes for the first time in over a decade.

Music is an incredibly powerful pathway. We can recall exact moments in our lives by playing music associated with them. Remember your first kiss? Was there music playing? I can remember summer camp between 4th and 5th grade, slow dancing to *In Your Eyes* by Peter Gabriel and sneaking kisses when we thought the camp counselors weren't watching. Muscle memory is similar — we can do a physical routine, play an old instrument, or dance an old dance, and suddenly, we are transported back to that time and place. We *feel* it.

What creates these powerful associations? Intense emotions actually lock memories in — the more you enjoy or dislike something, the deeper the memory goes. The more you enjoy it, the more likely you are to remember the details in an accurate, positive, and useful way. The more you dread something, the less you will recall it clearly — the memory will be focused on your emotions instead of the details.

Listen to music that makes you joyful, excited, and happy to be alive. Be very aware of the lyrics. Some songs may sound happy or uplifting, but the lyrics might be awful — you'd be surprised how often this is the case. Make sure to keep things positive — your subconscious hears everything, and as Marisa Peers has taught us: your subconscious is your body, doesn't understand sarcasm, and follows your thoughts and words as best it can. If we think negative thoughts, we are sending signals to our body to degenerate or to do the opposite of what we'd actually like. We'd like to be less overweight, but we keep saying: I can never lose weight! It's like a mantra that our bodies hear and obey. Music acts similarly: we can be keying in the code for either enthusiasm or depression.

Dancing is invigorating. By raising our heart rate and elevating our breathing, we feel the reality: we are ALIVE!! We exist because our hearts continue to beat and we continue to breathe! There is a joy that can come from exercise, but not always. Dancing is different — it almost always is associated with joy. Dave Jerden, the music producer, once told me that Brian Eno, Dave's mentor, had a rule that a mix was only done when he found himself dancing. The song had to be so good that it caused spontaneous dancing — bubbling joy that shakes its way out of us as we move.

Singing songs that bring us peace and joy has long been a proven method for finding our enthusiasm in the darkest of times. Singing unites us, keeps us focused, and can even transform hardship into faith. When we raise our voices in sincere song, we open our hearts and unleash our deepest enthusiasms. Sing loud and sing proud — your heart deserves to sing free.

Art & Creative Expression

> The purpose of art is to create enthusiasm.
> ~Pablo Picasso

Whenever I felt low or lacking purpose growing up, I would turn to art, at first it was drawing and poetry and later it was music, but it was always creative expression that would bring back my enthusiasm. As a child, I would lose myself for hours making art. For several years after I'd graduated, I told people my best friend in high school was my bass. Today, I color to reconnect and find writing books and telling stories to be one of the key ways I cultivate my enthusiasm and share it with others. It has always been my therapy, but at first, it was very personal. Art, as a practice, invariably draws us out of our shells to share the beauty we've found in our exploration. It heals us and then brings that healing back into the fold, so we all can grow from your growth.

What can we do today to increase our creativity? Meditate? Use our hands? Color? Draw? Write a song? Paint? Carve? Sculpt? Design? It is up to you. There are many ways to increase our creativity through art, play, and meditation, but all require you to practice and ideally in a way that abandons time and the outside world. If we can lose ourselves in the creative process, we will find our unstoppable enthusiasm.

Service

When we look outside of ourselves, we immediately recognize the overwhelming need for service in our world and local communities. There are youth, elderly, and everyone in between that need a helping hand, a kind word, or a friend. It may be they need help moving in, shoveling their driveway, carrying their groceries, or stacking firewood. They may need advice on parenting, starting up a small business, or overcoming addiction or trauma. The needs are great, and in service, we become great.

When we provide service to those in need, in that moment, we are the answers to sincere and heartfelt prayers. It's an incredible responsibility, and when we are caring for those that desperately need it, and they express their gratitude unfeigned, it can be overwhelming — we overflow with that connection of gratitude, faith, love, and joy.

This is the true difference between the unstoppable enthusiasm I write of and the taxing, and sometimes enthralling enthusiasm that extends into mania. Unstoppable enthusiasm extends, not into mania, but into joy where we are overwhelmed by emotions of love, tears of joy, and deepest gratitude. Mania implies a disconnection from others and a disregard of ethical boundaries — being connected to the divine in ourselves and the divine in those around us is the opposite of mania. Service at its best reminds everyone involved that we are all one family and deeply connected.

When we provide service in our community with enthusiasm, we do more than donate time, prepare food, or serve a meal, we give those in need meaning and purpose. We reconnect them to their enthusiasm, gratitude, and connection to life. A smile, a patient ear, encouragement, and compassionate words can turn a life around.

Saying I Love You

Many of us grew up not hearing *I love you* or *I'm proud of you* enough. Many of us heard *you're not good enough* or *that's not good enough* so many times we internalized it, and it became confused with our own thoughts. Meditation is a great way to begin to label these thoughts and rewrite them. We can also take charge during our day with affirmations and psychological cues, but what's more is we can just start saying *I Love You* more: to ourselves, to the people around us, and to our environment. Now don't get yourself in trouble here — you might say you love this or that about that person or the way they worked on something instead of telling people in an open-ended way that might confuse them. In the English language, we lack separate words for parental love, sibling love, friend love, spousal love, and love of a good meal — it's all umbrellaed under one term, so misunderstandings are common. When we speak this phrase, we are wielding a very powerful social agreement, so use it wisely and with care but use it as much as you can. Cultivate sincere love and express it every chance you get, and the world will reciprocate.

Connection & Community

While it can ignite communities and convert masses, enthusiasm can also be sparked by community and connection. We can go to a local gardening group's weekly meet-up and come away supercharged with enthusiasm for the upcoming growing season. You might be low from the daily grind and need to get together with friends and go dancing to reignite your passion and joy for the moment. You might find your Sunday worship to be the time you recharge. You may get inspired just sitting among the crowd. You might interact, you might even lead, or you might serve quietly on the sidelines. This, again, is up to you, but it is an incredibly powerful way to spread and supercharge your enthusiasm.

Therapy vs Self Improvement

Are you working on fixing something wrong or are you aiming beyond equilibrium to something far greater than an absence of a problem but the product of overcoming that challenge? Therapy is usually to fix something and does not usually go well beyond repair and into high performance. It's important to understand where we are in our progression because these two concepts overlap and are sometimes confused. Therapy is needed when we cannot help ourselves; we need help from a professional in a 1:1 context. This book can absolutely be used alongside a therapy program, but it is not a replacement for a medical professional working with you 1:1. This program is ultimately about training our unstoppable enthusiasm for nonstop self-improvement. We are overcoming our challenges ourselves — the techniques in this book will help you craft your best life, but it is your work that is making it happen. This is your victory, your big win, and your best self.

Supplements & Food

How can food and supplements have anything to do with enthusiasm? Our food actually directly influences the genetic expression of our cells. MicroRNA are very small molecules that are not broken down in digestion, but instead, travel to the cells directly and interact with the cell membranes themselves. In simplest terms, food is information we are sending to our cells, and it is also what we source to continuously regenerate our bodies. We are what we eat, but we also feel what we eat. Foods can make us happy, depressed, anxious, and energized — make sure you know what you are eating has been grown or raised to nourish you. Most food that is available is less than what it could be. Long term studies have shown that our food is losing its nutritional value, and while we can use permaculture and regenerative organic agriculture to turn things around, we are still likely to need supplements to account for the lack of nutrients, especially minerals, in our food. I say *likely* because Joel Salatin's family might not need to take supplements: Polyface farm's food may be nutritionally dense enough because they regularly supplement the soils with healthy compost and minerals, but it would depend on individual digestion and blood work to know for sure. Few of us have the luxury of living on a regenerative organic farm on par with Joel's, but we all can choose cleaner, fresher, and more local, native foods — consuming the best food has a natural tendency to help us feel great which naturally lets our enthusiasm flow. Many of us have not tasted our best peach yet, but when we do, we'll have the profound epiphany that food itself in its pure exquisiteness can bring unadulterated joy, surprise, and enthusiasm.

What supplements? What are you deficient in? Speaking with a nutritionist, a naturopathic doctor, or an informed medical professional, getting our levels tested, and keeping a food journal for a while can tell us a lot about what we need. Soon we will be able to use an app on our phone to do the same testing with only our cameras. That being said, there are universal recommendations that also can be powerful. Dr. Daniel G. Amen, a brain health expert, recommends vitamin D, omega-3, saffron, SAMe, probiotics, DHEA, regular saunas, and more water to boost our brain health which supports our overall health and sense of well-being — both of which are critical to feeling unstoppably enthusiastic. There are also supplements like Restore that work to provide some of the missing nutrition we'd be getting from healthy foods grown in healthy soils. The word used on the bottle to describe its contents is *terrahydrite* i.e. liquid earth. For me, it has been instrumental in my healing my gut. You might need supplements too, temporarily or for an extended period of time, but each is individual, so follow your enthusiasm, get expert feedback, and treat yourself to the best nutrition.

Immersion in the Natural World

"The work soon became so all absorbing that I have continued it with undiminished enthusiasm all these years. No words can convey the least idea of the intense enjoyments, the almost countless thrills these winter studies have afforded me"

~Bentley, snowflake photography

Mentioned earlier as part of the Daily Ritual section, contact with the natural world stimulates deep enthusiasm, wonder, and joy in many people. Though for many of us, we do not have a daily touchstone of nature in our lives. You may need to make it a top priority to make it out into nature once a week if it brings you joy. You might switch careers to be closer to the ocean. You might enlist your family and start hiking together in the national forest.

It's worth it — consider how much it cost the indigenous peoples of North America. When the bison, Tatanka, were hunted nearly to extinction, the indigenous peoples lost the touchstone of their enthusiasm — so much so, that singing among them ceased. The bison were central to their culture, their seasons, and diet. With over 120 million bison at the time of first documentation, they roamed from northern Mexico to deep into Canada. The bison visited innumerable cultures and bioregions and were cherished everywhere. We can bring back the bison migration loop and revive our loving relationship with the natural world. While some may not feel an emotional or heart-based connection with the natural world, we are of that world, and our health, bodies, and energies are intrinsically tied to that world. Much of our madness, sadness, sickness, and turmoil are rooted in deprivation of regular participation in natural processes.

Growing up in New England, the winter blues always hit me hard. Recently, I have stopped having seasonal-related depression even though I live in the Pacific North West, the darkest region of the USA. I take vitamin D supplements pretty regularly, but whenever the sun does come out, I stop what I'm doing and bask in it. Maybe just my face or my hands — sometimes it's just a few rays but the warmth and regeneration it brings are precious and sweet.

Sepp Holzer, the bear-like Austrian agroecologist, is known for napping, basking in the sun amidst a thick profusion of garden and wild plants. My younger son, Oliver, does this as well. I realize now it's a form of meditation really where the focus is on the feeling the sun gives us and gratitude for it. Oliver calls them his Sun Spots. Right now as I write, there's a beam of light coming through the trees and shining on my left arm. I routinely duck down and put my face directly into the stream with my eyes closed. The instant warmth and glow of the sun are singular and powerful. There's a deep recognition that we are of the sun, we are creatures made of light, and when we bask in the sun, we bask in the light of our creation. Refreshed and renewed, we are filled with deep resonant enthusiasm.

Newness

New experiences have the ability, in general, to spark our enthusiasm, gratitude, and wonder. My wife, who grew up overseas, is at her most enthusiastic and joyous when she is traveling and visiting somewhere new. She thrives on it! Routines, room layouts, outfits, hairstyles, dance moves, movies, and even relationships: newness has our attention! In fact, we get a dopamine release both when we seek and when we experience something new — interestingly, the seeking releases more dopamine than the finding, so it creates the desire to search for more and more new things. This is why we get hooked on scrolling on a news feed on social media or go on a Netflix binge. We get locked in a dopamine seeking-rewarding loop, but is that where we want to end up? Knowing how this works can help us avoid being caught staring vacantly at our thumbs rubbing the screens of our cell phones or some other addictive behavior. Instead of plugging ourselves into empty novelties, let's feed ourselves authentic, new experiences with real people in real places. It will keep us learning, expanding our repertoire, and avoiding stale patterns.

Changing up our ritual using the menus is all about keeping the freshness in our daily lives, but sometimes we need a deeper newness. Traveling to a foreign country can absolutely accomplish this, but so can reading a new book, taking a class in something you are unfamiliar with, or meeting new people. Open yourself to the newness all around you. If we can sincerely feel grateful for this moment, we will see everything for the first time again.

Learning

How many books are you reading per week?

On average I'm reading two books a week, but sometimes that's just one, and other times, it's four or five books. I'm reading physical books and listening on Audible to audiobooks. I'm also reading articles online, in magazines, and in journals — as well as watching Youtube, FoodMattersTV, and Vimeo. I'm also enrolled in or have access to dozens of online courses. At any moment of the day I can be learning, and I love to learn. It brings me intense joy — I love constructing and expanding an organized understanding of the world.

Some people have mind palaces or other memory tricks, but I incorporate everything I learn (that is of value) into an organized framework from micro to macro. This is how I teach permaculture and how I have such a good memory. I don't quite have my mom's photographic memory that allowed her to quote legislation and law word-for-word including the line and page, but I've found if I'm enthusiastic about something, I don't forget it. I've also found if I study what I'm enthusiastic about I don't forget what I study. You might say, this sounds unique to you Matt, but I didn't have a great memory until I quit drinking and began to find my path to enthusiasm and to feel more centered in my life. From what I've seen in the classroom, in the research, and in my own life: if it brings you joy, you won't forget it. You will remember it with joy and excitement, anticipating the next opportunity to do it again or learn more! It's pure and natural — let your enthusiasm and curiosity flow!

Witnessing Enthusiasm

Last but certainly not least, most of us have experienced enthusiasm as a witness. We were watching a movie, reading a book, at a live concert, at church singing, playing a sport, or listening to a speech or talk, and we were swept up by the enthusiasm. We left that moment charged with enthusiasm, but over time, it dissipated. While it is important to build enthusiasm that is generated from within, using triggers that help us get back on track or amp up our enthusiasm are invaluable.

I have certain songs, videos, talks, words, and memories that are triggers for my enthusiasm. My mirror trigger affirmations bring me enthusiasm for instance, but so does rewatching Fred Rogers in *Won't You Be My Neighbor* or listening to *Can't Hold Us Back* by Macklemore & Ryan Lewis. I'm sure yours are just as individual and diverse. Maybe when you're really stuck, you're watching Goalcast or Impact Theory Youtube videos on repeat, until you feel reconnected and alive. Maybe it's learning from an enthusiastic teacher, but whatever it is, gather what makes you enthusiastic and surround your life with those reminders.

Imagine Yourself…

You're unstoppable. You're feeding your enthusiasm throughout your day, morning and night, and now you are branching out: exploring the world, sharing experiences, and diving deeper into what makes you enthusiastic. Every day feels like an adventure. You've got life by the tail, and you're ready to ride it. You've unleashed your inner artist, athlete, and poet — you're cracking your code and going for gold. Every day you wake up feeling more and more empowered with enthusiasm.

Enthusiastic Action Menu
Take Action & Make It Happen

Deliberate Practice

Asking Questions

Enthusiastic Walking & Talking

Dressing the Part

Enthusiastic Play

Exercise & Sports

Singing, Music, & Dance

Art & Creative Expression

Service

Saying I Love You

Connection & Community

Supplements & Food

Immersion in the Natural World

Newness

Learning

Witnessing Enthusiasm

Download & Print It Out:
www.matt-powers.mykajabi.com/p/unstoppablereaders

Enthusiastic Thinking

If we aren't thinking enthusiastically, we can fall into the trap of just doing the motions. The emptiness, the mindlessness, or, even worse, the dread we might be incorporating into our bodies when we do things without enthusiasm are dangerous — keep your mind clean and clear of negativity with enthusiastic thoughts.

> It's Possible!
> ~Les Brown

Everything invented was once a thought in someone's mind. If we don't think it's possible, it never will become a reality. We have to have faith in ourselves, in our dreams, and in our thoughts. If we can have the self-confidence to enthusiastically believe in ourselves, we carve out a door in life that no one else can walk through. If you want an extraordinary life bejeweled with moments of joy and enthusiasm, start with your mind. From the seat of an enthusiastic mind, anything is possible.

Being Present

When we are enthusiastic, we cannot help but be epically HERE in the moment. We don't need to seek peace or to be one because we are already in the zone. We are so excited that those around us perk up and try to understand what there is to be learned. Your presence sparks their curiosity and it draws them out into the present with you. We can cultivate this skill through meditative practice and exploring our enthusiasm.

Compliments

Honoring and praising others enthusiastically is like tossing your excitement around the room — it's infectious and people start getting enthusiastic! Their smiles reach the corners of their eyes, and you see all their teeth! While it technically is an action, compliments are generated from a mindset that sees a world waiting for a compliment, needing praise, and wanting support. How can we honor people in how we think about them? How can we think more complimentarily about the people around us? When we think the best of the others, we give them the space to be their best selves. When we share what we see as the best in others, we increase the likelihood that they will enjoy, continue, and expand those behaviors.

Laughter & Humor

> Against the assault of laughter nothing can stand.
> ~Mark Twain

Of all the pathways an argument can take to resolution, laughter is the shortest. Humor can unlock forgiveness and empathy with a suddenness unlike anything else. If we can only laugh, we can transcend the most difficult of situations. If we can laugh, we can let go of stress and the hidden weights we've been carrying. We transform under the spell of laughter — it's also contagious.

The surprise of humor and the release of laughter opens our minds to the possible. It also improves memory and powerfully connects us to the moment. It's considered one of the best medicines. Laughter boosts the immune system, releases t-cells, lowers blood pressure, improves blood flow, and prevents cancer growth. Some even say it has been instrumental in healing from cancer. Laugher releases oxytocin, dopamine, and endorphins — it lowers pain and boosts our energy. Because it heals, supports, and energizes our brains and immune systems, laughter naturally supports higher performance.

> The smartest people in the world I know are the funniest.
> ~Anthony McCarten

My laugh has changed over the course of my life significantly. I can clearly recall my laugh being called *annoying* when I was young. I think my self-consciousness and uncertainty as a person leaked out in my laugh and made other folks uncomfortable. I've always sent out strong signals — positive or negative, I've always had an effect on those around me. Recently, I was told that I had an amazing laugh, their favorite laugh ever, and this wasn't the first time this has happened, but all of these spontaneous laughter compliments have come about in the past two years. I believe it has to do with healing myself and finding myself. Laughter is healing, yes, but it is also revealing. We can hear the edge of despair or a cry in the laugh of someone nearing the end of their rope. We can hear sincerity, mania, enthusiasm, and delight all in a laugh.

Being silly is also very powerful though doesn't seem like it superficially - the reality is being silly is a sign of defiance: the negative realities though harsh and painful cannot hold your spirit back from accessing humor, fun, and freedom from that pain. It's also a humor that doesn't seek to degrade another person's value in any way — this is critically important to me as I find almost all humor these days to be focused on making fun of someone else which is a real shame. When people around me are in pain (or when I am in pain), I find myself invariably becoming more silly to compensate — and not in a way that disrespects their suffering but, instead, invites them with a kind smile to open a window and let some of their suffering air out.

Anticipation & Curiosity

In many ways, enthusiastic thinking is rooted in excited anticipation of future events: it is gratitude for something that hasn't happened yet. That in many ways is the key to enthusiasm's power: our brains cannot tell whether or not it has happened yet. We revel in the possibility and, in tandem, increase the probability of it really occurring. Also, it should be noted that we don't have to be anticipating anything in particular: the thrill of uncertainty is very real and has its own form of anticipation and enthusiasm. We are all curious in our own way about our own things, but how can we leverage that into the way we think on a baseline level? The same way we are building our enthusiasm: practicing and thinking about what stirs our anticipation and curiosity in a habitual fashion. If you spend any time studying enthusiastic and brilliant scientists, you'll find their curiosity carries them forward onto the next project like a conveyer belt. If we study what increases our curiosity and, thus, anticipation, we will increase our enthusiasm in tandem.

Curiosity = Always a Student

To be a life learner is to be ever curious. To let your enthusiasm lead you on from challenge to challenge without dimming, only increasing in intensity. It's an approach to life — we are actively humble, listening, and seeking truth and understanding about ourselves and our world. Being happy and reveling in knowing that we can never know it all gives us the power to continue ever onward on our own journey into the unknown.

> Curiosity in some ways is the opposite of judgment, you can't hate something if you're curious about it, and really you can be curious about everything.
> ~Hank Green

Just like how gratitude pushes out negative emotions, curiosity has the ability to flip our mindset into growth. Curiosity is a superpower for overcoming hardship — we shift our focus to our intellectual hunger, and we let go of judgment, the past, and pain. By asking questions, we feed our curiosity, and by playing into the dopamine seeking-rewarding loop, we increase our curiosity: one question leads to another or several more. We can very quickly create momentum to our enthusiasm and curiosity if we learn to ask the right kind of questions. When we are sincerely curious about those around us and when we compliment them, very shortly, they are curious about us too. Follow your curiosity, and it will lead you to the most interesting places and connect you to the most interesting people.

What can this teach me? How can we always be teachable? Always look for the lesson even in the worst of situations. We are always learning even in despair and anguish — even when we are making mistakes, we are learning what not to do! Sadly, many of us have become experts in depression and anxiety through personal experience, but we can substitute that miseducation with something that will uplift us. It all starts with our mindset and perspective. Look for empowering learning and you will find it. Enthusiastic people naturally are teachable and open to learning — they are students of life and ever curious.

Acknowledging Grief & Pain

Enthusiasm is not the denial of grief or pain. It's not an escape from or the containment of suffering, but it is a way of letting go — we allow ourselves to shift our focus to the spark that burns within us for more meaning in our lives. In order to do this, we have to acknowledge the pain, we don't have to dwell, but we have to acknowledge: that is pain, that is suffering, that is guilt, etc. When we name them instead of trying to flee from them, we get back on track faster. We also position ourselves for growth by accepting what **is** in preparation to decide what **will** be. Like laughter, enthusiasm can pull us out of despair and help us feel alive again.

Acknowledging the Negative

Often when we take the time to recognize our pain and suffering, we get stuck stewing over it. How do we avoid that? It's important to make sure we don't shift from acknowledging the negative we encounter in our lives to seeking it out — it's only a scroll or click away on any device these days. Judgment and negativity can both be addictive — we have to protect ourselves from negativity in all forms, but how? Through enthusiasm, we can find a path and protection.

When I was in high school, I encountered a teacher that changed my life. My dorm parent and later history teacher, Phil Peck, was always happy, kind, and genuinely enthusiastic, so much so that I found myself asking him questions, curious to know if he was positive from lack of understanding or from a deeper perspective of life. Up until that point I'd accepted that ignorance was bliss — the more you learned, the more miserable you were. Phil Peck seemed to openly defy this as he discussed Russian and Chinese history, conflict, atrocities, everyday challenges, and his own personal struggles. He approached it all with the same bright can-do attitude. After spending years learning from Phil, I understood: he knew both sides of the story but chose his perspective to align with his faith rather than allowing the stories he encountered to dictate his perspective. He didn't let new information unsettle his inner world — his faith was a sure foundation. Because Phil had the understanding that God loved him, he was able to navigate the negative armed with a positive perspective, faithful that good could still be found. It didn't matter if bad things happened, he was determined to continue to spread positivity and kindness in the world.

> People are often unreasonable, irrational, and self-centered.
> **Forgive them anyway.**
> If you are kind, people may accuse you of selfish, ulterior motives.
> **Be kind anyway.**
> If you are successful, you will win some unfaithful friends and some genuine enemies. **Succeed anyway.**
> If you are honest and sincere people may deceive you.
> **Be honest and sincere anyway.**
> What you spend years creating, others could destroy overnight.
> **Create anyway.**
> If you find serenity and happiness, some may be jealous.
> **Be happy anyway.**
> The good you do today, will often be forgotten.
> **Do good anyway.**
> Give the best you have, and it will never be enough.

> Give your best anyway.
> In the final analysis, it is between you and God.
> It was never between you and them anyway.
>
> ~Mother Teresa

Spirituality: Something Greater Than Ourselves

For Phil and for me, acknowledging that we are part of something greater than ourselves, something that connects us all, and something that stirs the heart has allowed us to overcome many challenges. In Alcoholics Anonymous, having a higher power is one of the 10 steps: *Why?* The 9th form of intelligence is Spiritual though it is often labeled the unknown intelligence in academia. Spiritual intelligence is the ability to find meaning in the world around us, and that is what gives each of us purpose in life. We are all more enthusiastic when we can have reverence for those around us, for the world, and for ourselves.

When we lead with our enthusiasm, we also connect those around us to the joy of creation. We are nature, we are born of creation, and so we are part of the whole expression of creation. When we completely infuse it with enthusiasm, life is at its fullest, most alive, and most sweet. We celebrate life with our very being.

We may have a personal practice, a cultural tradition, or a local group we meet with, but we all benefit from spirituality, from finding meaning in the world around us. It gives us resilience when nothing else can. It gives us hope, meaning, and purpose as well as a way to serve, connect, and be vulnerable.

Total Commitment

There is an undeniable commitment to true enthusiasm. That enthusiast has 100% faith in their new invention or idea — they are betting everything on it. No matter the odds, the enthusiasts are fully committed to seeing it through. Even when we are losing, we have faith that good will come of it.

Even if we are not facing hardship, enthusiasm has the ability to propel us into commitment. Decisions are made as if by instinct — answers come as if we've already had time to consider the questions: the vision carries us through it all, and sometimes, we never even touch the ground.

> Commitment is staying true to what you said you would do long after the mood that you said it in has left.
> ~Inky Johnson

Commitment also acts as a guard rail in our lives — when we have lost the emotional thread, but we stick to our commitments, we only need ask one question to bring us back to our enthusiasm and the original reason we decided to make the commitment in the first place: *Why is this important?* When we make commitments rooted in our enthusiasm and as we honor those commitments even in the hardest times, the integrity that is generated by this will allow us to always reconnect with our enthusiasm. We just have to remember. We just have to ask *WHY*.

> I play to win, whether during practice or during a real game. I will not let anything get in my way of me and my competitive enthusiasm to win.
> ~Michael Jordan

Being Open

Perhaps seen by some as naive, enthusiasm is more accurately being open to possibility. Being open is also about being honest, transparent, and willing to share from the heart. Enthusiasm naturally leads us to this place — it is a place of fearlessness. This openness makes us unstoppable.

TMI? Do you get negative feedback from your closest friends and family about how open you are? They act as if it's their personal life you are sharing not your own, right? *What's with that?* It takes immense courage and confidence to be enthusiastically open. It makes us vulnerable to attack and in that we demonstrate that we are even more powerful and unstoppable because we are unafraid of judgment. Don't be held back by others fear or definition of who you are: be open and follow your heart.

Being Okay Being Wrong

Enthusiasts bounce; they do not break. Their mistakes are how they learn and the fuel that launches them to the next insight and discovery. For many of us, being wrong is embarrassing and shuts us down, but if we could rewire this to be something we can learn from, we will begin to be okay with being wrong.

Quick to Forgive

Enthusiasm helps us be quick to forgive — we don't have time to dwell on the past, we are focused on our future, we are full of faith, and we are deeply grateful to be on this path. In being unstoppable, we recognize that others aren't going to get it and may even try to stop us without understanding why — in their own way, they are trying to figure out what it is that makes us so relentlessly proactive and positive, but it's usually through an attempt to exert control over what we are doing or even to disrupt us. Enthusiasts forgive these people because we see them for what they are: looking for their own enthusiasm. That's why we forgive them and share our passion for life, speaking from the heart.

There is a playfulness and child-like openness to enthusiasm that is also disarming. This is how great and terrible leaders of our past have been swayed by those equipped with unstoppable enthusiasm. It's also how a chained husky turned a polar bear keen on eating it into a new playmate. When we bring enthusiasm to life, we let go of the mistakes we make as well as those made by others — the past doesn't have a hold on us; enthusiasm holds us too strongly in the present.

Unstoppable Enthusiasm Indicators

There are very clear signs when we are exuding Unstoppable Enthusiasm — everyone around can recognize it in us, but sometimes we have a hard time gauging how unstoppable our enthusiasm really is. While there are many indicators of enthusiasm, there are specific, unbidden traits that typify the state very clearly — they are also, like enthusiasm itself, contagious:

- *Spontaneous Laughter* - How often are you laughing in pure delight?
- *Spontaneous Dancing* - Just like Brian Eno, when we are joyous, we dance!
- *Spontaneous Singing* - Like dancing, singing is an energetic joy that just bubbles out of us. It can bring humor and more laughter to the moment.
- *Spontaneous Smiling* - *What are you smiling at?* Have you ever been asked that? When we are enthusiastic and unstoppably so, we will smile more than normal and even smile for no reason — people around us will notice!
- *Gratitude for Gratitude, Enthusiasm for Enthusiasm* - Are you able to feel grateful for gratitude? Can you be enthusiastic about enthusiasm? It can feel like a brain teaser at first, but this, once mastered as a habit, creates an unstoppable engine for your life.

Imagine Yourself...

Your mind is filled with enthusiastic thoughts! You have the mental energy to creatively approach any situation. You're ecstatic to be you and in this moment. You laugh, smile, sing, and dance spontaneously. You can direct your thoughts to ramp up your enthusiasm, and you can even be enthusiastic about being enthusiastic. You are in full control of your enthusiasm; you are UNSTOPPABLE!!

Enthusiastic Thinking Menu
Time to think about thinking!

Anticipate Good Things

Be Present

Freely Give Compliments & Accept Them with Grace

Think the Best of People Around You

Laugh More & Look for the Humor

Be Curious — Always be the Student

Acknowledge Pain & Grief

Acknowledge the Negative

Increase Your Spirituality

Get Totally Committed

Be Open

Be Okay Being Wrong

Be Quick to Forgive

Download & Print It Out:
www.matt-powers.mykajabi.com/p/unstoppablereaders

Bouncing Back

The worst bankruptcy in the world is the person who has lost his enthusiasm.
~H. W. Arnold

Maintaining perfect enthusiasm for a prolonged state is often difficult or impossible, especially at first — life has a way of interfering with our plans, so where does the unstoppable part of Unstoppable Enthusiasm come from? The only way to ironclad your enthusiasm truly is to have it rooted and centered in peace, the kind that comes from within, from compassion, from listening, from acceptance, and from gratitude. It is not something we can force though it can protect us from very strong forces that would otherwise destabilize us.

So, what can we do?

There are two paths: avoidance and, when that becomes impossible, acknowledgment. Avoid those things that take your enthusiasm and acknowledge when it does happen, so you are free to work through it. Sounds simple enough, but let's look closer.

BEWARE Enthusiasm Drains

There are so many things that drain one's enthusiasm — fast or slow, their effect is the same. We are left tired, disillusioned, and aimless. We don't know what to do, so we flip through our phones, check our messages, and check out which, of course, further drains us.

Some of these drains, you will recognize, and some, you might not. Social media, your cellphone, your email inbox, messenger, Instagram, Facebook

— they all drain you even as they entertain you, but I bet you didn't expect some of your friends to be drains too? The friends that complain, worry, posit negative conspiracy theories, use their language aggressively, exist in a self-definition of struggle, blame others, and seek easy answers will drain your enthusiasm. We all get stressed, but how we deal when that stress defines us and affects everyone around us. Can you find uplifting content on Youtube, Instagram, your inbox, or your cell phone? You sure can, but there are also studies that show high performance is directly correlated with avoiding using our phones and social media an hour before bed and an hour after waking. The technology has a time and place. The inbox will eat your day, your mind, and your peace. Beware social media, technology, and bad influences — no matter how subtle they seem to be in the moment, the aggregate effect over time is a drain on your enthusiasm and a derailment of your purpose.

It is important to note that worrying is the opposite of enthusiasm. Worry is fear, a wariness of future potentials, a profound lack of excitement and faith. Worries, when acknowledged, can become incredibly powerful turning points. If we let our worries chase us, we will feel out of control, but if we let solutions swallow those concerns, we turn those fears into wisdom. It is important to ask ourselves consistently: *Is this true?* and then honestly answer. We often share the same fears as those around us, those we influence, and those we are influenced by. When we overcome them, we open a path for others to do the same. Seeing these moments of derailment as opportunities to grow in a way that serves our best selves and the greater good allows us to transcend them and inoculate them with enthusiasm and courage. Now, this is in the case of legitimate fears and worries, but what about the garbage — the stuff you KNOW doesn't belong there and cannot help you in the slightest?

Any self-violating behavior, thoughts, or entertainment will drain your enthusiasm. It cuts you off from the spirit within and leaves you hollow:

When we watch something we know we shouldn't,
When we entertain thoughts we would never say aloud,
When we act in ways we wouldn't want others to witness,
We cut ourselves off from our enthusiasm,
We stop ourselves from taking the higher road, and
We lose a constellation of positive possibilities

Negative self-talk puts holes in our boat, but everyone has these A.N.T.s as Dr. Daniel Amen calls them. A.N.T.s stands for Automatic Negative Thoughts. We all have them, but when we accept them as our own and when we feed them our fears or desire, we fall prey to them and they will take EVERYTHING from us if we let them, so SQUISH THOSE A.N.T.s!! (Please be good to real ants as best you can!)

What puts those A.N.T.s in there? Often the entertainment we take in has something to do with it: are the characters facing conflict? Are they modeling positive self-talk and mindful actions? We become what we take in, not just our food, but with our eyes and ears. Listening to depressing music does not lead to uplifting emotions — it may not make your abjectly depressed in one listening, but it doesn't charge you with a passion for life. In fact, music like that sort represents a call for help. If you are listening to that kind of music, there's something in you that needs attention. There's a wounded area that hears that music or reads that book and finds solace in it because it mirrors your pain which is fed by a negative, disempowering story, but could someone steal your enthusiasm?

BEWARE Enthusiasm Thieves

Different from drains, these thieves are individuals in our lives that can rob you of your intention in a moment. These folks may be worried about your safety, or they may even enjoy distracting you with their endless debates. That Interrupter might just be bored. The Negative Nancy might feel better about their own problems when they contrast how risky your latest endeavor is.

Protect your enthusiasm from the negativity of others.
~H. Jackson Brown, Jr.

There are some folks who will try to break you down, to steal your momentum, or to get a quick boost from bringing you down, but don't let them. They are always a small crowd, but they're always vocal, and we're all likely to encounter more than a few times in our lives. Protect yourself — remember why you are enthusiastic and hold to it tightly. Therein lies our path to being unstoppable.

Be Aware of Enthusiasm Killers

Health crises, the death of a family member or friend, job loss, a fall from grace, the loss of a talent or ability, or war, these attack the very roots of our enthusiasm. We know it is possible to maintain enthusiasm in the face of loss, but often when facing it ourselves, many, if not most, of us quickly lose our footing and fall prey to despair, anger, or fear. We can grieve without falling into despair. We can face adversity with courage and love.

When we are sick, it can be very hard to muster the enthusiasm to do much more than drink water and rest. While we can do our best when we are sick to find our enthusiasm, it may not come so readily. I've found giving ourselves time to heal is necessary. Just like when we've spent an entire day at a high level of enthusiasm and we are exhausted when it comes time for bed, we are too tired to connect or fire that part of our brain properly. We need energy for enthusiasm, and it comes from our physical body in large part. Give yourself and others time to recover their spark for life when they're facing health challenges or a lack of sleep. Enthusiasm is linked to growth, but when we are healing that same energy gets routed towards healing. Stay positive, maintain your habits as much as you can, and rest — in time as you heal, your full spectrum of energy will return.

When we are faced with great loss, we also need to take time and honor the process. You may find in acknowledging the loss you can move forward, but sometimes we cannot. Sometimes we lose part of ourselves that we were relying upon for our identities like a business or a marriage, and our enthusiasm needs to travel deeper into the why behind what that loss used to bring us. It may be as simple as a need to love and be loved, to serve the community, to work with children, to solve difficult problems, or to share spiritual messages. Beneath the pain from our loss, the love can still be found, and if we can reconnect to why we love, we can find our enthusiasm again.

BEWARE Counterfeit Enthusiasm

Brendon Burchard often cites the old RaRa days where motivational speakers would get their listeners ramped up into a frenzy of manic energy. The results were quick wins (for the motivational speakers), but did it last for their audiences? The results speak for themselves: participants felt a short-lived boost of confidence, clarity, and energy. Positive thinking is powerful, but it needs to rest upon something to sustain it. It needs to be what internally excites us and gives us peace — that is truly unstoppable enthusiasm, and it is a state that is recognizable, stable, trustworthy, and abiding. We must be wary of faking it to making it — don't get up from your meditation until you feel it. Don't write until you feel it, until you have tears, joy, excitement, or inspiration flowing. Does that mean don't write every day? That means we need to figure out how to call upon that state and maintain it, so we can write when we have the time to write. Does that mean I'm perfect and "always on"? Nope. I have to wait sometimes, meditating, for the heavy feelings to pass and be replaced by feelings of lightness, enthusiasm, and peace, but it always comes. It's always there waiting inside us: there's always something to be enthusiastic about. We just have to open ourselves to possibility, to the authentic enthusiasm within us all.

Feel the peace. Feel the welling of enthusiasm within you. Breathe.

SHARE With Others

Often the hardest thing to do is be open when we are hurting or to ask for help when we are feeling worthless. It feels impossible, counterintuitive, and counterproductive: *How can sharing help us get back on track?* Sharing is central to almost all forms of therapy. Doctors and therapists try to relax their patients and gain their trust, all in order to get them to start sharing. Once they begin sharing, change can begin. We might answer our own question or let the emotions run their course. The other person might give us the insight we've been needing all along or remind us of a piece of the puzzle that only now makes sense.

For some folks, they already know that sharing is the way they learn, heal, grow, and problem solve, but for many of us, we avoid it, and the cost is great. We are held back by our lack of sharing — don't let this happen to you. Reach out to those you trust and share when you are low, lost, or in need of a boost. It may not resolve your trouble, but it will give your mind some ease and open you up to more possibilities as well as enlist people you trust in your struggle.

Accept We ALL Say Crazy Things We Don't Mean

Where did THAT come from?
When the moment is charged with emotion, we say what we don't mean: *Why?* To win, to be right, to lash out, to show how deeply we feel hurt, to persuade, to hurt… but does it work? Does it help at all? It may if we can laugh at ourselves in the moment or at least pull back, apologize, and

retract or reconfigure the statement, admitting we are wrong. Perhaps it's a way we unconsciously make a mistake on purpose, so we can admit we are wrong, so we can pause and change course in the midst of an argument. Letting go of the crazy things people say to you, or even do to you, while they forgive you for your own lapses is the key. What's more important is that we reset, get back in touch with who we really are and how we really feel, so we can get back on the right page with that person or group of people. We all have off days and times, but forgiving each other, letting things go, and moving forward is how we get out of the funk.

REST REST REST

Are you getting seven to nine hours of sleep for days and weeks at a time? Are you going to bed every night by 10 pm? Our circadian rhythms are powerful cycles that cannot be overlooked, and if you are looking to heal and reset, you need to get a full night of sleep consistently for days, weeks, and even months. Rising early and having the headspace for quiet reflection is vital.

This may mean taking a nap - *like right now*, just stop what you are doing and go lay down. A twenty to sixty minute nap might give you exactly the reset you've been needing. When I was a professional touring and recording musician in New York City, I spent most of my time working and learning from Saturday Night Live's house drummer Shawn Pelton. Shawn was a master at catching a nap at any time of day and in almost any situation: the recording studio couch between takes, in any vehicle, on any plane, and during any waiting time period. He was serious about fitting in the sleep, and I pointed it out one day, and he said he slept when he could so he could be ready for anything at any time. Often Shawn would be gigging until the small hours of the morning, sleeping only a few hours, and then moving on to the next gig. Shawn's ability to quickly shift from sleep state to performance level enthusiasm was also incredible — Shawn always focused on playing at a performance-level of enthusiasm, and after seven years playing with him in all sorts of contexts, I never heard him play without the electric snap of enthusiastic joy! I learned a lot about performance enthusiasm from Shawn, but now that I reflect more on my time with him, I recognize that he also focused on a constant meditative state of rest. He managed his energy, so his enthusiasm was always ready when it was time to perform.

You may also be slightly sick or even exhausted which manifests itself in so many different subtle shades. I get a cold every time I don't rest enough. I sometimes get irritated or physically sore as well, and I'm not as patient or resilient when I am not getting enough rest. Give yourself the time to heal, reconnect, reflect, and grow.

Reframe

How can this tragedy be seen as a challenge? If we can reframe the situation and see with a growth mindset instead of through the lens of our pain, we can circumvent our strong emotional reaction and focus on solutions and bringing enthusiasm back to the moment. Sometimes this is characterized as *being objective* or *being unemotional*, but I disagree: it is a way of suspending our negative, defensive, fear-based reactions, so we can engage the full range of our being and choose our reaction from the full spectrum of options. Being open to the situation's needs and what will truly serve us is our focus when we reframe.

REMEMBER Ourselves

> I can do more. This just can't be it…
> There's something in your heart…There's something in you that tells you this is not it for you.
> ~Les Brown

You're going to forget... everything — not all the time, nor permanently, but you will have times when you wake up and forget the new you, or something will happen to trigger an old habit or a burst of irritation. You wake up angry, sore, confused, or groggy, and you default to the old you, throw out your neck, or return to an old habitual attitude or perspective. Someone cuts you off, cheats you, or talks negatively about you behind your back. Maybe even good friends turn against you and spread lies about you. It is going to happen to some degree — it's not a matter of if but when. You may not have the world end, but you may say something you didn't mean. The only way to deal with it is to prepare ourselves by doing the work to develop our enthusiasm like a muscle, so we can flex it out of memory in our times of greatest need.

Mentioned at the start of the book, I had an IndieGogo campaign fail to make its mark to start a physical, in-person school in Sebastopol, California, *the Permaculture Life School*. It was the last weekend of the failing campaign, and I felt exposed, embarrassed, devastated, and overextended. I felt like everyone was watching me fail. Our family had moved into a single room for a limited span of time, gone into debt, and risked it all to try to start a school with very few resources. Now, failure was apparent, a giant tipi was already being shipped to us, and the majority of the money we'd raised, I'd already spent... on the giant tipi. How was I going to turn this around? How was I going to find the lesson in this? I felt foolish, but I also knew that nothing of benefit could come from that space. I let go of my reaction to the pain and began to pour that same energy into answering questions like *How can I fail upward? How can I turn this into a success in this moment?* The pain wasn't gone, but I couldn't dwell on it; I had to move on. I knew something *had* to happen — my back was against the wall, and the only way to find a way forward was to look within. Two days of soul searching, and I had it! My school's mission was to share permaculture education with children, but all my backers were online and none were locals who could have signed up for the actual school. I realized I wasn't speaking to the right audience, but they were still receptive and supportive. I already had the demand; I just wasn't serving them properly.

Once I realized this, I envisioned my own online course, designed the entire thing on paper, and launched it within days without even filming the course itself. It was a completely bold leap of faith, and it ultimately launched my career in online education. It was backed by over 40 students, and I filmed, edited, and released it week by week. Because I was able to snap out of a disconnected state and back into enthusiasm, I was able to bounce higher than I fell in the first place. I wasn't working with 18 students in Sebastopol as I was aiming for — now, I had over 40 students with the possibility of exponentially more, and I had a lot more freedom.

What do you stand for? What makes you tick? What lights you up? Who are you when the chips are down? Remember who you are and step into your greatness, your unstoppable enthusiasm.

What if you've lost the thread of your enthusiasm?

We're going through the motions and exercises like a person rifling through piles of paper looking for the right one and bordering on the edge of panic. Doing the exercises may not instantly return us to our prior state. We might be sick, hurt, or facing some other hardship in real-time. We can feel empty and lost, a shadow of our former selves, but keep at it. You will bounce back — just keep up your routine and enthusiastic habits, and you will remember yourself!! This happens to me whenever I get really sick. I lose my voice, creativity, and energy — it is like having my batteries taken out, but it's happened to me so many times now that I know I will come back to myself again. I just have to keep moving forward in faith and that part of myself will catch up at some point down the road — it may only take hours, but it may take days, weeks, or even months, but remembering ourselves is not only possible, it's the only path towards our best self and best life.

Remember Others

When we are feeling low or out of sorts, one of the best ways to get ourselves out of that place is to serve others. *How's everyone else doing?* Remembering our mission can also help us come back to ourselves: *Who are you doing this for?* How are the people in your community and close relationships feeling? What are their needs right now? What are their dreams, and how are they progressing? What can we do to help them achieve their goals? Can our smile make their day brighter? Are we serving them with our negative thoughts, our hesitancy, or even inaction? The opportunities around us are endless, and when we get involved, we leave behind our own problems.

Steven Covey shares an experience in *Seven Habits of Highly Effective People* about a man with rowdy children on a train. From the moment they entered the train together, it was clear the children were his, and it was even more clear they were out of control. The other people on the train were quickly frustrated with this man. The father sat next to Steven Covey on the train and was oblivious to the chaos his children were creating. Fighting irritation, Covey asked the man if he was going to step in and control his children. The man was startled from his stupor and looked about as if seeing the situation for the first time. The man told Steven Covey they'd just come from the hospital where their mother and his wife had just died. Immediately, Steven Covey's irritation was replaced with compassion and sympathy. The entire scene changed before his eyes. Remembering others can transform the moment as quickly as thought.

Forgiving others is also a form of remembering them — we don't know where others are in their lives and what they are currently facing, but we can let go of the past as we recognize the unmet needs their behaviors indicate and, perhaps, as we recall mistakes we too have made. Making service a part of our day every day will always keep us connected and help us return to ourselves when we are down. Serve in your community. Serve in your family. Spread kindness every chance you get. Give gifts wherever you go — even if it's just your presence.

Remembering We Are Loved

In every setback, there's a setup waiting to happen
~Jake Olson

Along the same lines as having faith, remembering we are loved by people in our lives and by creation itself can give us peace, comfort, insight, a boost, and resilience in the darkest times of our lives. We are born out of love and come from a long legacy of love — even if it seems those things are distant from us now.

We are enough. We are worthy of love, and we are loved. Let that love shine through.

Make the Routine NEW AGAIN

Focus on the process — enthusiasm is about the PROCESS more than the results though it's important to celebrate and internalize all our wins. Remember: we are happy just being here and exploring the possible. We need to keep our routine fresh and that takes focusing on the process with a commitment to go deeper, further, or longer. It might mean slowing down to make things new again or changing it up — that's why I provide all the menus. You might approach it with curiosity to keep it fresh or push yourself every day towards that *1 More*. Whatever it is for you, do it: don't let things get stale!

Letting the Idea of Control Go

It can often be the most painful thing to let go, the thing we are most afraid of doing, and where we are most tender: our sense of control. When we let go of trying to control the world around us, we are freer. When we focus on controlling our thoughts, emotions, and behaviors, we open up a world of choices in life we never realized we were skipping over. Self-control rather than external control is a great relief — we no longer have to try to control the uncontrollable: other people and life itself. Life can throw our way what it will; we will react as we choose, and we won't be dictated by life's circumstances nor try to control them.

Let Enthusiasm Back In

So many times, we push away the opportunity to reset because we are *still mad* or *still hurt*. We hold onto that pattern in our minds, playing that neural pattern over and over, re-experiencing the pain. It can feel hard to let the enthusiasm back in, but we need to in order to heal. You might just need to go for a walk or watch a motivational Youtube video, and then again, you might need to go talk to that person to move forward, but do what you need to do to remove what is holding enthusiasm back from flooding into your heart.

At times like this it becomes clear that enthusiasm is truly En Theos - *the divine in me*, because when I'm without enthusiasm, I'm lost, blind, and lacking in faith — faith in myself, others, and possibility. When I'm back in enthusiasm, it's like a light switch gets flipped on. There's a flood of electricity, connection, and life. Let yourself feel again the fire and passion you had when you began this journey.

Say It Like You Mean It
If you're off track, it is powerful to use your affirmations from the first moments of your day after a meditation or nap and to not allow yourself to

progress from affirmation to affirmation until you can feel the words emotionally. Continue until you feel your enthusiasm return.

Imagine Yourself…

You've been through hell, but you've come out the other side. You're so grateful to have healed, to be reunited, to be back. It's taken so much to bring you out of that situation that you are now forever changed — the experience has made you exponentially more committed to your mission. The setbacks have turned into life lessons and made you wise. The heartaches have opened you up and allowed your heart to expand. You are back and better than ever — *You have Unstoppable Enthusiasm!*

Bouncing Back Menu

What to do when you are mad, sad, or feeling apathetic

Beware Enthusiasm Drains, Counterfeits, & Thieves

Be Aware of Enthusiasm Killers

Share & Ask for Help

Accept, Acknowledge, & Forgive

Rest Rest Rest

How Can I Reframe This?

Remember Who You Are

Remember Others: How Can I Serve?

Remember You Are Loved

Keep It Fresh - Make Old Things New!

Let Go of Trying to Control the Situation

Let the Enthusiasm Back In

Download & Print It Out:
www.matt-powers.mykajabi.com/p/unstoppablereaders

One Last Thing
(Maybe Two)

Enthusiasm = Action

We are using excitement, gratitude, and anticipation to give us energy but then balancing that with faith and mindfulness habits — we are building a repertoire of sustainable, resilient enthusiasm. Once it develops into a muscle we can rely upon throughout our day, we now have regenerative enthusiasm that is resilient, self-healing and constantly spreading — this is Unstoppable Enthusiasm, and with it, we can take action and be the change we want to see in the world.

Without enthusiasm, action is nearly impossible. It is as if you are actively trying to prevent yourself from accomplishing your task. It is like a dead weight within you is generating an inertia of hesitation and doubt. Options seem to have equal weight and crowd in, confusing you. Without enthusiasm, we cannot stick to it. We invariably trail off, peter out, and quit.

Using this book, we can uncover and reconnect to what makes us enthusiastic. Train your mind for enthusiasm and action will always follow!

Forced Growth vs Tender Growth

Often there is a temptation to force ourselves.

We fake it until we make it.

We push through the pain and grief.

We break past our barriers.

Forcing is often like a child's early learning - it's rudimentary or sloppy, will-based, and lacks control and finesse. It is high intensity and drains our energy quickly. I do not suggest this route for adopting the ideas in this book. I've done it both ways and have learned a few things, but first, allow me to use one last story to illustrate this point.

My entire life I've wanted to be able to sing like a rockstar — like Freddie Mercury, but I just have never had the ability. I tried forcing my way through every style and copycatted them to my best ability but each sounded strained. I would try screaming like Kurt Cobain and get a great recording but be unable to sing the same way live for a thirty to forty-minute set. Forcing my voice only left it weaker the better it got.

Only when I gave up singing and playing music professionally did my voice, after a decade of daily warmups, begin to take shape. This entire time, I've been working on letting go of force and allowing my actual voice to surface. For many of us, our enthusiasm is the same way. It is a voice we never learned or a pattern we lost touch with at some point. It is the gentle and graceful strength that we never had a chance to develop, but we still can.

It is not an easy path, but it will open our most tender areas to growth — these areas once strong are what we call our best qualities and highest callings. They are also our personal touchstones for enthusiasm.

You No Longer Have To Imagine You Are Unstoppable Embrace Your Greatness & Let It Engulf You Totally

It is my deepest desire that you find your path to deep and lasting Unstoppable Enthusiasm!!

Grow Abundantly, Learn Daily, & Live Regeneratively,
~Matt Powers.

"Enthusiasm is one of the most powerful engines of success. When you do a thing, do it with all your might. Put your whole soul into it. Stamp it with your own personality. Be active, be energetic, be enthusiastic and faithful, and you will accomplish your object. Nothing great was ever achieved without enthusiasm."

~Ralph Waldo Emerson

Continuing Your Education

Unlocking Your Enthusiasm, *the Free Course*
Included in your purchase of this book is a 3-part course on finding and unleashing our greatest power: our Enthusiasm! Join Matt Powers in this fun and inspiring introduction to Unstoppable Enthusiasm!!

Start Today: https://matt-powers.mykajabi.com/unlockyourenthusiasm

Other Books by Matt Powers
Available on Amazon, Barnes&Noble, & ThePermacultureStudent.com

Regenerative Soil

Regenerative Soil Microscopy

The Regenerative Soil Teacher's Guide

The Permaculture Student 1 set also available in Spanish, Arabic, French, Italian, and Polish!

The Permaculture Student 2 set

The Advanced Permaculture Student Teacher's Guide

The Regenerative Career Guide

5 Steps to a Regenerative Future

The Magic Beans

Permaculture for School Gardens

Other Courses by Matt Powers
All these courses are available on ThePermacultureStudent.com

Permaculture Gardening with Matt Powers

The Permaculture Student Online K-12

The Advanced Permaculture Student Online

Regenerative Entrepreneurs & Experts

References

There are a lot of books that influenced this work, but I wanted to highlight the very best by author to get you started on furthering your research.

Burchard, Brendon. *The Motivation Manifesto* (2014). *High Performance Habits* (2017). *The High Performance Planner* (2018).

Dispenza, Joe. *You Are The Placebo* (2014). *Becoming Supernatural* (2018).

Duckworth, Angela. *Grit* (2016).

Dweck, Carol. *Mindset* (2008).

Eisenstein, Charles. *The More Beautiful World Our Know Is Possible* (2015).

Graziosi, Dean. *Millionaire Success Habits* (2017).

Hampton, Janie. *How The Girl Guides Won the War* (2010).

Pool, Robert, & Ericsson, Anders. *Peak* (2016).

Rosenberg, Marshall. *Nonviolent Communication* (2015).

Shimoff, Marci. *Happy For No Reason* (2008).

Acknowledgments

Thank you to my wife and two boys who put up with me as I again plunged into writing a new book. Thank you Adriana and Mike for editing this book with me. I love you all so much.

Thank you to my extended family, friends, peers, and mentors who inspired, guided, and listened to me throughout my journey. I would have been lost without your help along the way.

Thank you to the amazingly supportive and loyal Kickstarter backers who made this book and all my books possible.

I thank you all for facilitating my dream to help people everywhere live their best lives, so all may have the opportunity to love and be loved.

Grow Abundantly, Learn Daily, & Live Regeneratively,

~Matt Powers

About the Author

Matt Powers is an author, educator, and entrepreneur focused on radically transforming the K-12 experience for children everywhere by aligning their education with current regenerative science, natural principles, and clear ethics: earth care, people care, and future care. Through Matt's collection of online courses, teacher's guides, textbooks, and workbooks, K-12 students can understand collegiate and graduate school concepts, learn how to ethically redesign our world, and even restore and rewild large landscapes, reversing the devastating effects of climate change. Matt's work is found in English, Arabic, Polish, and Spanish with a dozen more translations currently in process. Matt's bold vision is to empower children everywhere to live in regeneration where every action and decision are beneficial to the local and greater ecosystemic and social community. Matt is a former public high school English teacher with a masters in education.

www.ingramcontent.com/pod-product-compliance
Lightning Source LLC
Chambersburg PA
CBHW052037070526
44584CB00016B/2080